OUTLAW TALES
of Kansas

OUTLAW TALES
of Kansas

True Stories of the Sunflower State's
Most Infamous Crooks, Culprits, and Cutthroats

Second Edition

Sarah Smarsh

Continued by Robert Barr Smith

TWODOT®

GUILFORD, CONNECTICUT
HELENA, MONTANA

A · TWODOT® · BOOK

An imprint and registered trademark of Rowman & Littlefield

Distributed by NATIONAL BOOK NETWORK

British Library Cataloguing-in-Publication Information available

Library of Congress Cataloging-in-Publication Data available

ISBN 978-1-4930-1676-1 (paperback)
ISBN 978-1-4930-1677-8 (e-book)

∞™ The paper used in this publication meets the minimum requirements of American National Standard for Information Sciences—Permanence of Paper for Printed Library Materials, ANSI/NISO Z39.48-1992.

For Kansans, who reached the stars through difficulty.

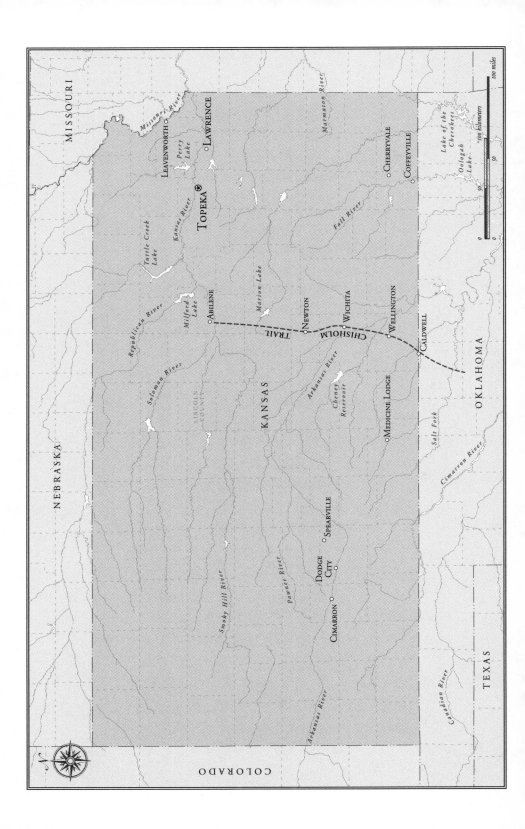

Contents

Acknowledgments

Thank you to the Kansas State Historical Society and photograph curator Nancy Shubert for their careful assistance and to the Center for Kansas Studies at Washburn University for its research support.

Introduction

In its early years, Kansas was the handbasket in which some of the most famous outlaws of all time rode to hell. The home of Dodge City, Abilene, and a host of other dangerous outposts, Kansas was a wild place that harbored wild people. From menacing packs of robbers like the Dalton Gang to solo sociopaths like John Hardin, outlaws terrorized Kansas despite the best efforts of lawmen like "Wild Bill" Hickok and Wyatt Earp.

From the start, Kansas was perfectly positioned for violence and mayhem. Smack-dab in the center of the country, white settlers established the Kansas Territory in 1854 (to the near-destruction of native peoples and cultures). The next few years were marked by fiery battles over whether Kansas would be a "free state," as was the inclination of many abolitionist settlers, or a "slave state" like neighboring slave-holding Missouri to the east. The issue sparked savage, deadly border wars between Kansans and Missourians. Known as "Bloody Kansas," this period was a traumatic childhood of sorts for the young Kansas Territory. The border battles also served as training for famous outlaws, many of whom learned about bloodshed in the years before and during the Civil War. Kansas finally joined the Union as a free state amid national chaos in 1861, the year the Civil War officially began.

In coming years, it would be Kansas's neighbor to the south—lawless "Indian Territory"—that allowed for considerable headaches. Robbed a train? Murdered a bank teller? Just escape across Kansas's southern border and find refuge in the ungoverned red-dirt nooks and crannies of Indian Territory (which would not become Oklahoma until half a century after Kansas's inception).

In yet another geographical twist, Kansas in the late nineteenth century found itself split up the middle by the Chisholm Trail. The trail, that untamed route on which gun-toting cowboys drove cattle north from Texas to the Kansas stockyards, was a constant target of gun-wielding cattle rustlers. And, as posts along the trail, the Kansas towns of Abilene, Newton, Wichita, and Caldwell saw their saloons overrun by rowdy cattle drivers given to drinking, gambling and, sometimes, killing.

Of course, Kansas outlaws have existed outside the realm of the "Wild West." But those formative years of heated politics, unruly cattle trails, and proximity to Indian Territory made nineteenth-century Kansas a fine home for outlaws—and one of the most violent places in our nation's history.

Bushwhackers
Gunslingers in Training, 1863

The quiet, unnoticed approach. The sharpshooting. The take-no-prisoners attitude. The fast escape. The most infamous outlaw gangs of the Wild West had train robberies and bank heists down to a science. So how did they learn the business of being outlaws?

Jesse James and his older brother, Frank, were just children when their homeland started going crazy. They lived on their family farm in Clay County, Missouri, a stone's throw from neighboring Kansas, and in the 1850s saw the state border erupt in violence. The conflict was over slavery; Missouri was a "slave state," the Missouri Compromise of 1820 having allowed for legal ownership of slaves (the James family held slaves on its farm), and Kansas was a territory teeming with abolitionists who wanted to enter the Union as a "free state."

Guerrilla warfare from both sides—"Jayhawkers" from Kansas and "bushwhackers" from Missouri—terrorized the border area during the years before and during the Civil War, leaving dead bodies and burned-out buildings in their wake. Though the Union and Confederate armies attempted to bring these militants into their folds, many bands remained off the grid, making their own rules and following their own questionable codes of conduct—killing civilians and unarmed soldiers, robbing individuals and businesses, burning homes to the ground. Often their methods seemed less to do with political ideology

1

than with a thirst for violence. And by their teenage years, Frank and Jesse James were right in the thick of it.

In the spring of 1863, at the age of nineteen, Frank James joined a group of bushwhackers in ambushing pro-Union factions in Missouri's Clinton and Clay Counties. They murdered their prisoners before going into hiding on the farm of Zerelda and Reuben Samuel, Frank's mother and stepfather. Union forces caught wind of their location and descended on the farm, beating Frank's fifteen-year-old brother, Jesse, and choking Reuben

Artist's depiction of Quantrill's raid on Lawrence, Kansas. *Kansas State Historical Society (Pen-and-ink drawing; artist Lauretta L. Fox Fisk)*

in a noose. The stepfather gave in, leading the men to Frank's hiding spot in the woods. Several died in the ensuing gun battle, but Frank himself escaped across the Missouri River.

This humiliating assault on the family, combined with the Emancipation Proclamation and major Confederate losses at Gettysburg and Vicksburg, lit a fire in the James brothers. Young Jesse soon would join the bushwhacker ranks. In the meantime, Frank fell in with militia leader William Quantrill.

On August 21, 1863, Quantrill led four hundred men, including Frank and future famous outlaws Cole Younger and "Bloody Bill" Anderson, across the state border into the abolitionist enclave of Lawrence, Kansas. In what would be known as Quantrill's Raid, or the Lawrence Massacre, they slaughtered more than two hundred men and boys and torched nearly every business in town.

Frank and Jesse's mother, Zerelda Samuel, was so proud of her son's participation in the slaughter that she named a newborn daughter Fannie Quantrell [sic] Samuel.

The Union's response to the massacre was to order the evacuation of ten thousand border-county Missourians, whose homeland was promptly devastated by retaliating Jayhawkers. The Civil War was unofficially being fought by enraged mobs, some of which included the murderous likes of the James brothers.

Frank James spent the early winter months of 1864 with Confederate bands in Texas before returning to Clay County, Missouri, in the spring. His sixteen-year-old brother, Jesse, joined the group in time to embark on a homicidal spree. The group went house to house, slaying farmers who sided with "the North."

One Missourian wrote of the outlaw secessionists, "A general terror prevails. Today there is not in the county of Clay one unconditional loyal Union man who dares to go into the harvest field to do a day's work. Many of them have left the State; all are now talking of going."

Frank and Jesse's group directly encountered Union fighters a few weeks after their rampage on rural citizens, and their leader ended up without a right arm. So the James brothers hitched their wagon to another merciless Southerner, William "Bloody Bill" Anderson. Anderson had parted from William Quantrill's gang with around fifty of its most ruthless killers, picking off unarmed citizens and soldiers as they roved the countryside.

When Frank and Jesse joined, the crew made its base at the Samuel farm, where Zerelda and her meek husband did their best to once again hide their boys. Knowing the Samuels were among the most dangerous families in Clay County, the Union attempted to remove them from the area, to no avail.

In September 1864 Bloody Bill led the James brothers and about thirty others into Centralia, Missouri, where they yanked twenty-two unarmed Union soldiers from a train, shot them dead, and then made a display of their mutilated bodies. When militia attempted to run them out of town, Bloody Bill's gang—which had picked up more bushwhackers in Centralia—killed another 124 men, again engaging in grotesque mutilations. One member of the band and a mentor to Jesse, Archie Clement, was known for cutting the scalps from victims' heads and hanging them from his horse's bridle. After this atrocity, even the Confederate army—which unofficially condoned much guerilla warfare, as did the Union—wouldn't take Bloody Bill's fighters into its midst when General Sterling Price led a Missouri invasion.

The next month, Union militia leader Samuel Cox managed to ensnare Bloody Bill in an ambush and kill him. Seeking vengeance, Frank and Jesse James went on another tear through Clay County, slaying any last Unionists they could sniff out of private homes before running south.

Their mother of course would not give up their whereabouts when questioned. Union Captain William Kemper wrote in a report that Zerelda was "one of the worst women in this State. She has two sons in the brush now & have been for 10 months. They have engaged in the murder of a number of citizens of this county. They were with Bill Anderson and assisted in the murdering of 22 unarmed federal soldiers at Centralia Mo some time in the month of Sept last. I heard her asked the question a few days since, if she was not ashamed of her sons—the way they were acting & she rejoined that she was not—that she was proud of them—that she prayed to God to protect them in their work. . . . It is not through anything personal that is existing between these parties & myself that I speak thus. . . . I feel today that I am almost as much in 'rebellion' here in this county as I would be in South Carolina."

Reuben and Zerelda Samuel finally were run out of Missouri in January, settling just across the Missouri state border in Nebraska.

The war ended in the spring of 1865, but bad blood between North and South still flowed as strong as ever. One Union officer reported in the fall of 1866—more than a year after the war's end—that western Missouri still harbored packs of gun-toting militants. Indeed, a gunfight had taken place that summer near the Jameses' childhood home. The officer called it "a habit which grew out of the unsettled condition of the country since the war." It was a habit that Jesse James would never give up.

After Bloody Bill's death, Archie Clement inherited the top spot in the James brothers' band and took the group in a whole new direction: bank robbing. The outlaws' well-honed battle skills would come in handy in a bank heist.

In February 1866 they held up the Clay County Savings Association in Liberty, making off with $60,000 and accomplishing the country's first armed bank robbery in broad daylight. It was no coincidence that the bank was run by former Union fighters. For Clement and the James brothers, the Confederacy's loss was an open wound.

During the months that followed, the guerrillas-turned-robbers knocked over more banks, all owned by Unionists. They also threatened political enemies as the fall election drew near; many Union people lived in fear.

On Election Day, Clement, Jesse James, and company essentially overtook the town of Lexington, Missouri, to ensure the election of conservative candidates. Clement wound up dead and full of bullets in front of a saloon, and Jesse was shot in the chest. Though he survived, Jesse was arrested in Lexington—and then somehow paroled. He was left even more bitter over the loss of his bloodthirsty hero, and ten years later would write that "Arch Clement, one of the noblest boys, and the most promising military boy of this age, (was) murdered in cold blood (by) Tom Fletcher's cut-throat militia." Jesse's mother named a new son Archie, in honor of her son's fallen mentor.

For the coming years, Jesse and Frank both would gain national reputations as menaces to banks and trains across the country, stealthily evading the lynch mobs that snared so many of their former bushwhacking compatriots.

Though Frank was famous in his day, Jesse was the brother who would gain not just infamy but veritable support among former Confederates who viewed him as an avenger of sorts. He painted the banks he robbed as part of the Federal system that had stamped out the Southern way of life, though most agree he was just as motivated by his growing lust for riches.

Just as Hollywood Westerns have painted Jesse as a populist hero, so too did many papers of the time. The *Kansas City Times*—edited by John Newman Edwards, a former soldier for the South—ran stories and commentaries sympathetic to Jesse and his crimes. To many defeated Confederates, Jesse wasn't a sociopathic thief and killer but rather a hero, a bandit, even a Robin Hood who redistributed the Union wealth (though, in reality, he only redistributed it to himself).

In December 1869, five years after Bloody Bill's death at the hands of Union militia leader Samuel Cox, the James brothers still held a powerful grudge over the killing. While holding up the Daviess County Savings Association in Gallatin, Missouri, Jesse shot and killed a bank officer he believed to be Cox. Reports of the day state that Jesse yelled, "This is for the death of Bloody Bill Anderson!"

The vengeful act likely was the real motive for the heist—the boys left without any money.

A lot of things went wrong that day, not the least of which was that Jesse killed the wrong man. The cashier was not

Samuel Cox after all—just a man who resembled Cox, who worked as a cashier in a similar-looking bank in the same town square. Then, as the James brothers made off on horseback, Jesse fell from his horse and was dragged along, tangled in the stirrup. He managed to free himself and, abandoning his own purebred horse, hopped onto Frank's.

En route to their hideout, the James brothers happened upon an area farmer on horseback. The man's horse was a good-looking one—strong, with four white feet and a white mark on its nose. It was just the sort of horse that might hasten the James brothers' getaway—so they pulled out their guns and stole it.

Turns out, they picked the wrong farmer to mess with. The man filed a lawsuit against the James brothers, seeking damages for the stolen horse, saddle, and bridle. The brothers hired a top-rate lawyer, who successfully had the case dismissed on a technicality. But Jesse James wouldn't let a dead horse lie. He wrote a letter to the *Kansas City Times*—whose editor was a friend of sorts—declaring his innocence in the Daviess County heist and murder. He claimed that the horse abandoned near the bank had been sold to "some Kansas Jayhawkers" and thus didn't prove his presence at the scene of the crime. He even boldly invited a proper trial.

Meanwhile, the farmer's lawyer again brought suit regarding the horse theft; the Jameses' attorney objected, but the brothers insisted on letting the matter go to court.

They lost.

The wronged farmer was awarded more than $200, in addition to the high-dollar horse that Jesse had left behind. It was the first and last successful civil suit against the James brothers in a time when few would challenge the fearsome duo. In fact, the young prosecutor representing the farmer would dodge several of the Jameses' bullets.

Now Jesse had been officially linked by the horse ordeal to the bank robbery and cashier's murder. So surely he would be tried and convicted, right?

That's where the battle lines drawn during the Kansas-Missouri border wars would once again come into play. Daviess County officials were former Confederates who held the James brothers in high regard. They had no plans to try Jesse and Frank for the robbery or murder. At the state level, though, Union sympathizers would step in. The governor offered a $3,000 award for turning in the James brothers, now at large. Two brothers who had murdered and terrorized Kansas Jayhawkers, as well as abolitionists in their own state of Missouri, had become politically polarizing figures. To Unionists they were immoral thieves and cold-blooded killers. To Southern sympathizers they were wily bandits who refused to recognize a Federal system that had stamped out their way of life.

In the coming years, as the nation began to heal the wounds caused by the Civil War, Jesse and Frank James wore out their roles as Confederate avengers. By the late 1870s Missourians were tiring of their guerilla tactics and slower to defend their heists across the country.

In 1882 Jesse James was killed by an associate, Robert Ford, who collected a $10,000 bounty from the Missouri governor. Dying young, on the heels of nearly two decades of infamous violence, meant that Jesse would become a legend of the West. Southern sentiment again flowed in favor of the Jameses' criminal antics. Frank, tired of running and defeated by his brother's death, soon turned himself in. He was tried in Missouri and Alabama for robberies and murders. Surprise, surprise: He was acquitted.

Johnny Hardin
Teenager with a Gun, 1871

On an August night in 1871, eighteen-year-old Johnny Hardin—wearing nothing but his underpants—jumped from an Abilene hotel balcony. It was time to get out of town. Hardin had only been in Kansas for a few months, and he had just killed his eighth man there.

His blood-soaked stay in the state had begun that spring when he led a large herd of cattle to Abilene from his native Texas. But killing was nothing new to Hardin. Though he was just seventeen when the cattle drive began, Hardin's bone-chilling body count already was fifteen men, including a freed slave he'd murdered in cold blood. Kansas, though, would mark a remarkably productive killing stretch for the dangerous teen.

Hardin, his fellow cowboys, and their sizable herd left Indian Territory and crossed the Kansas state line in May, veering from the Chisholm Trail on May 28 to have their fill of liquor and women in Park City. On the flat plains surrounding Wichita, they pushed across the Little Arkansas River and encountered a cattle drive from Mexico.

Hardin and the Mexican trail boss butted heads when their respective herds got mixed up. The Mexican man shouted for Hardin to get a move on and push his cattle more quickly; Hardin responded by inviting the man to pass the Texans with his herd. It was no small feat to move one herd around another, so

LAST BREAK IN ABILENE

John Hardin escaping the law in his underpants, as illustrated in his autobiography. *Kansas State Historical Society*

the Mexican trail boss cursed Hardin and collected his rifle. He took aim and knocked off Hardin's hat with a bullet. He then produced a pistol, firing menacingly as he approached Hardin.

Hardin's cousin and fellow cowboy, Jim Clements, ran to the scene as Hardin was attempting to return fire with an unreliable pistol. Clements came between the two men, imploring them and the alarmed cowboys to put down their weapons. A truce was called, and the two groups set up camp for the night.

But peace wouldn't last long. The Mexican trail boss had been nicked in the leg by one of Hardin's bullets and wanted revenge. He and six other men charged Hardin's camp. And Hardin was ready.

On horseback he shot the trail boss through the heart and then shot another Mexican man in the head. Then he and Clements nabbed two more men but, in a rare moment of pity, released them. Another gunfight ensued, however, and by the end of the ordeal, Hardin had killed five Mexican cowboys in southern Kansas.

The incident brought infamy to Hardin on the Chisholm Trail, where infamy was hard to achieve. The rough cattle-drive interstate was full of dangerous characters and wild stories, but a teenaged trail boss who had killed five men from another drive was a story worth telling. Many took to calling him "Little Arkansas," after the river where the gunfight had transpired.

Hardin and his herd rode into Abilene, where the Texas cattle would be loaded onto Union Pacific Railroad cars and shipped east. But Abilene was hardly all business. Cowboys, tired, hungry, and fresh off the trail, celebrated the end of their drives with inordinate levels of intoxication, gambling, and brothel visiting. Their wild presence called for serious law and order, and Abilene had hired Wild Bill Hickok as marshal just weeks before Hardin arrived.

Hardin's employers paid him to stick around in Abilene to watch over the herd until the cattle were shipped off. Earning a decent wage, he became a regular in the Abilene watering holes and brothels, where he commanded respect. There was nothing remarkable about Hardin's appearance—a modest mustache, a cleft chin, average build and height (about five-foot-nine) for the time—but his reputation had preceded him. During his time in Abilene, Hardin became well acquainted with Hickok, later claiming they were famous friends, and also came to know crooked saloon owners Ben Thompson and Phil Coe. Thompson and Coe had a heated relationship with Marshal Hickok—Coe eventually would be killed by Hickok—but Hardin and Hickok at least shared a mutual respect. They each were growing into living legends, their gunfighting prowess unmatched in their respective fields of law breaking and law enforcing. It's likely that they shared a drink from time to time. Still, it was Hickok's job to keep Hardin in check. On one occasion, finding Hardin packing two pistols in an Abilene saloon, he demanded that the boy disarm in accordance with a city ordinance.

According to Hardin's account, the young sharpshooter pretended to comply with Hickok's orders, producing both pistols with their butts facing the lawman. But then he showed off a fancy move—the "border roll"—quickly twirling both guns so that they were pointed at Hickok's head. According to Hardin, he proceeded to call Hickok "a long-haired scoundrel that would shoot a boy with his back to him," as unruly Texans shouted for him to kill the marshal. Hickok succeeded in talking the young man down, though, and the two shared a drink before noon.

Later the same day, a drunken Hardin killed a man in a restaurant saloon for cursing Texans. That made six victims in Kansas—and twenty-one in Hardin's short lifetime.

When twenty-two-year-old herd boss Billy Cohron was shot and killed by a Mexican drover during a heated argument, the Abilene cowboy population mourned. A funeral took place at Drover's Cottage, where most cowboys stayed, and the procession involved twenty-four carriages and thirty-eight men on horseback.

The killer, known as Bideno, had fled south toward his homeland, and prominent ranchers made it their business to make sure that the man was apprehended. They turned to the most famous shot of all the cowboys, John Wesley Hardin.

In early July, with horses and other resources supplied by the businessmen, Hardin and a partner left Abilene in search of Bideno. They rode for miles, picking up two helpers—including the dead cowboy's brother, John Cohron—along the way and stayed the night in Wichita. The next day they entered present-day Sumner City, just miles from Indian Territory, and split up to cover more territory. Having heard reports that Bideno was in town, Hardin fired his pistols to regather the posse. Hardin then sauntered into a saloon to discover that the fugitive was sitting in the restaurant.

"I called for drinks and took in the situation," Hardin later wrote. "I asked if we could get dinner and if a Mexican herder was eating dinner back there. They said there was; so I told my partner to get out his gun and follow me."

Hardin and his partner pushed through the restaurant door.

"Bideno, I am after you; surrender; I do not wish to hurt you and you shall not be hurt while you are in my hands," Hardin recalled telling the fugitive. Considering Hardin's past, his promise surely was a hollow one.

Bideno must have sensed as much, as he grabbed for his gun. Hardin was too fast, though. In an instant, he shot Bideno in the middle of the forehead.

After giving Bideno's hat to the murdered cowboy's brother, Hardin delivered a speech of sorts outside the saloon to inform the townspeople who had gathered.

Of course Hardin's account might be baloney. According to a newspaper in nearby Oxford, it was Cohron's avenging brother who shot Bideno in the head. At any rate, Hardin and his posse turned back toward Abilene, stopping in Wichita and Newton—where they may have shot up a brothel and raped its prostitutes—before receiving a hero's welcome for their successful mission. Hardin collected hundreds of dollars from the cattlemen who had put him on Bideno's trail. Including the five Mexicans at the Little Arkansas, and an unfortunate fellow in an Abilene saloon, Hardin now had picked off seven men during his brief tenure in Kansas.

There are two stories regarding the matter of Johnny Hardin jumping from an Abilene hotel balcony in his underwear on August 6, 1871, but they both involve Hardin shooting a man to death.

One story goes like this: Hardin and his cousin Gip Clements got ripped at the saloons and staggered back to their room at the American Hotel. In their stupor, the men fell onto their pillows and began to drift off. Then—and this is Hardin's version of events—a stranger slowly unlocked and opened the hotel room door. Through the darkness, Hardin saw a knife in the man's hand. He sprang for his gun and shot at the man. The intruder turned to run, but four of Hardin's bullets stopped him dead in the hallway. Unfortunately, for some reason the dead man had Hardin's pants in his clutches. Not wanting to emerge from his room to be seen rummaging about a bleeding body, Hardin slammed the hotel door to evaluate his options.

First, he felt certain that he had worn out any cozy feelings Wild Bill Hickok might have held for him. By then Hardin had contemplated killing Hickok and felt certain that Hickok had contemplated killing him. This latest incident, Hardin was sure, would cost him his life. The shooting might have been self-defense, but such details didn't matter at this point in Hardin's storied career as an outlaw.

The man in the hallway was discovered, and someone ran for Hickok. Soon Hickok and four policeman rolled up in a horse-drawn buggy. Hardin watched as the men ran inside the hotel. He knew there was only one way out.

"So in my shirt and drawers I told Gip to follow me and went out on the portico," Hardin later wrote. There they were, two young men standing on a ledge of the American Hotel in Abilene, one of whom wore nothing but his skivvies. Then Hardin jumped. His cousin followed.

The two men split up, with Hardin ducking into a nearby haystack as police began swarming about the outside the hotel. He then slipped into a cornfield and, seeing a cowboy happen by, stole the man's horse by pretending to have a gun in the darkness.

At this moment the police saw Hardin and galloped toward him on their horses. Hardin pushed his new horse for three miles to the river and then forced the animal to swim across. The police were still in pursuit, but Hardin felt strong and self-assured. He pulled away from the officers in the remaining five miles to a familiar cowboy camp.

"I was a sorry spectacle when I got to that camp," Hardin later wrote. "I was bareheaded, unarmed, redfaced, and in my night clothes." But he knew he couldn't rest yet. He found two pistols and a rifle, tucked himself into a hiding place, and waited for his pursuers.

Three of them arrived and asked the camp cook if he'd seen Hardin. The cook, Hardin's pal, lied and said he'd gone out to check on a herd of cattle. In the meantime, couldn't they use a meal?

The police sat down for a bite to eat. Catching them with their mouths full, Hardin crept up with guns in hand and demanded they drop their weapons. He then sent them back to town wearing nothing but their underwear.

A few days later, reunited with his cousin, Hardin fled to Texas.

The second version of the story is even more outlandish but perhaps the more likely to be true, as it paints Hardin as the heartless character he surely was.

Yes, Hardin and his cousin Gip Clements got drunk at the saloons, made their way back to a room at the American Hotel, and began to doze off. Then—and this is the accepted version of the event, documented in several newspapers of the day—a horrible snoring rattled through the thin hotel walls. Hardin couldn't fall asleep with such unbearable noise, despite the ample levels of whiskey pumping through his veins. He tossed and turned and finally arose and got his gun. Finally he fired at the wall until the annoying snoring stopped. Self-defense, indeed.

Hardin would continue to leave a trail of blood everywhere he went. On his twenty-first birthday he killed a deputy sheriff in Comanche, Texas, and his entire family was taken into custody in an attempt to ensnare Hardin. A vigilante mob stormed the jail and hanged Hardin's brother and two of his cousins. Hardin himself would prove much more difficult to hang. He was finally caught in Pensacola, Florida, tried for the deputy's killing, and sentenced to twenty-five years in prison. He served sixteen of them, in the meantime making several escape attempts and finding time to pen a factually strained autobiography. In it he detailed dozens of killings and attributed his interminability to one particular characteristic.

"Here I wish to tell my readers that if there is any power to save a man, woman or child from harm, outside of the Living God, it is this thing called pluck," Hardin wrote. "I never was afraid of anything except ghosts, and I have lived that down now and they have no terrors for me."

In 1895 Hardin's pluck ran out; he was shot to death in a dispute in El Paso, Texas. Upon entering prison, Hardin claimed to have killed forty-two men. Ironically, he died at the age of forty-two—a victim for each year of his life.

Phil Coe
Wild Bill's Nemesis, 1871

In the mid-1800s, Abilene, Kansas, was as close as a person could get to modern-day Las Vegas. Gambling, drinking, and altogether wild antics abounded. Saloons busted at the seams with rowdy, raucous cowboys playing five-card draw and fighting over their losses—or their women. The young, suddenly prosperous cattle town was overrun by cattle drovers, largely from Texas, who outnumbered permanent Abilene residents sixfold and had little regard for the laws of the town.

The *New York Tribune* wrote of Abilene, "Gathered together in Abilene and its environs is the greatest collection of Texas cowboys, rascals, desperados, and adventuresses the United States has ever known. There is no law, no restraint in this seething cauldron of vice and depravity." Feared gunslinger Johnny Hardin is said to have remarked, "I have seen many fast towns, but I think Abilene beats them all."

Gunfire in the streets, vomiting and passing out in the doors of saloons, rosy-cheeked and drug-addled prostitutes, outright thievery and murder—it was a cyclone of debauchery that the locals were hard pressed to stop, especially with guns pointed at them.

Town leaders convened in the spring of 1870 to pass an ordinance against carrying firearms within city limits. The edict was a joke to the wild drovers, who promptly shot up posters for the ordinance and ripped apart the town jail. The towns-people of Abilene needed help.

The same year the town hired a marshal purported to have served as a policeman in New York. The marshal, "Bear River" Tom Smith, was a tough enough character, known to ride up on his tall gray horse, Silverheels, and clobber heathens on the head. Unfortunately he only lasted four months. He was killed while serving a warrant on a pair of ranchers on Chapman's Creek in the fall of 1870. The city finally found a man as wild as Abilene itself—James Butler "Wild Bill" Hickok. He was a memorable fellow, with long, wavy brown hair past his shoulders, a handlebar moustache, and a decidedly grim expression. A former Union scout for General Custer's 7th Calvary, as well as an accomplished card player and a feared city marshal of Hays, Kansas, Hickok already was quite famous for his gun skills, honed as a child helping to protect his father's Illinois home—an Underground Railroad stop sometimes targeted by slave catchers. Famous lawman Wyatt Earp supposedly regarded Hickok as "the deadliest pistol shot alive," and stories of Hickok's marksmanship spread like wildfire—such as the one where Hickok fired ten straight rounds into a capital letter "O" on a sign in Kansas City, from one hundred yards away.

In 1867 Hickok had been profiled by prominent journalist Col. George Ward Nichols in *Harpers New Monthly Magazine*; labeling him "Wild Bill," the story greatly exaggerated the number of men Hickok had killed and sealed his role as a living legend, "the Prince of Pistoleers" in dime novels.

Hickok began as marshal of Abilene in April 1871. He quickly cleaned the place up, perhaps due to his reputation as having a deadlier draw than any outlaw. And while criminals feared him, local citizens revered him.

Abilene mayor Theophilus Little later wrote of a public school event celebrating the end of the academic year one May, where Hickok came to his rescue. Little, his wife, and two sons sat quietly watching the event proceedings, increasingly aware of "two big Texans" sitting in the seats in front of them. "They became very noisy and offensive and I remonstrated with them quietly, pled with them to keep quiet. They turned and laughed at me, asking what in 'h-ll' I was going to do about it anyhow."

Little eventually picked a fight with the two men and then feared for his safety upon heading home. "Just as the exercises close, Wild Bill strode swiftly toward us with his silk hat in his left hand, his right thrown across the left breast and with a low and courtly bow to Mrs. Little, in most gracious tones said, 'Mr. Little if you will allow me, I will walk home with you and your family this evening.' I thanked him saying, 'We would deem it an honor but not a necessity.'"

In Abilene Hickok regularly crossed paths with some of the most notorious figures of the frontier. Gunslinger Ben Thompson, for one, ran a wild saloon called Bull's Head Tavern, advertised with a sign featuring a drawing of a bull with an enormous, erect penis. At the townspeople's behest, Hickok had the sign removed.

By many accounts, Hickok befriended gun-happy outlaw John Hardin and was respected and obeyed by Hardin. Even the James gang, complete with the infamous Jesse, blew through town—though in this story, Hickok is perhaps less than righteous. According to a letter to a friend from Charles Gross, a room clerk at an Abilene hotel of sorts, the James brothers had

marshal at
Hays City
1869

"Wild Bill" Hickok, marshal of Abilene, in 1869. *Kansas State Historical Society*

done Hickok a favor during the Civil War. Perhaps they had spared the life of one of Hickok's Union friends? Perhaps they had killed one of his enemies in their role as guerilla Confederate soldiers? Whatever the case, Hickok supposedly repaid some debt by allowing the James gang to hide out in Abilene for a time.

It was this side of Hickok—this wildness, this ability to work outside the law though a lawman himself—that would get one Phil Coe into a lot of trouble.

Ben Thompson's saloon, the Bull's Head, was a growing operation at a central location in Abilene. Then his old military pal Phil Coe, who may have fought under Thompson in Mexico after the Civil War, came to town. Coe showed up in Abilene carrying lots of money and looking to make more, and the two partnered up in the saloon business.

Ben figured Phil would only increase the success of the Bull's Head. His presence was an attractive one: tall, early thirties, good looking, and confident. Coe had fought for the Confederacy for several years, surviving illness and battle with the 2nd and 36th Texas Cavalries. He had drifted from Texas to Salina, Kansas, picking up gunslinging and gambling tricks along the way. A raucous place like Abilene couldn't scare him.

Thompson and Coe made a killing with the saloon, and they developed strong relationships with the Texas drovers that locals viewed as riffraff and renegades. But when Thompson's wife was involved in a carriage accident that took her arm, his attentions were diverted from the saloon and Coe became the main man.

Wild Bill Hickok didn't like Coe from the start, and the feeling was mutual. The Bull's Head facilitated many of the criminal acts that Hickok was paid to curtail, and Hickok's patience with Coe wore thin. Some historians claim that the real root of conflict between Hickok and Coe was a quarrel over a woman, one Jesse Hazel. In one of the many Hickok legends, he stormed into the Gulf Hotel to find Coe and Hazel drinking wine. In an attempt to kick Coe, Hickok accidentally struck Jesse and then was thrown down the stairs by Coe—heating the bad blood between the two men to the boiling point.

In one famous verbal exchange, Coe reportedly boasted of his gun skills to celebrated marksman Hickok.

"I could kill a crow on the wing," Coe said.

Hickok responded coolly, "Did the crow have a pistol? Was he shooting back? I will be."

Whatever the cause of their mutual disdain, it would come to a head in October 1971. Rumors flew that Coe had pledged to kill Hickok "before the first frost," and tensions were high as the days grew shorter. The townspeople knew it wouldn't be long before one or both of the men erupted.

A cattle-drive was wrapping up, and dozens of Texas cowboys were reveling in the Abilene streets before heading back south. Hickok himself was enjoying a drink at the Alamo Saloon while keeping an eye on things. When he heard gunfire, he rushed outside to find Coe standing in the middle of the street, wildly firing his pistol in open defiance of the city ordinance. The streets were filled with carousing cowboys, and chaos reigned. Mayor Little later wrote that the madness of that night was orchestrated by Coe himself, "as vile a character as I ever met" who "sold whiskey and men's souls," for the express purpose of ending Hickok's life.

"For some cause, Wild Bill incurred Coe's hatred and he vowed to secure the death of the Marshall," wrote Mayor Little, to whom Coe apparently never repaid a $40 lumber debt. "Not having the courage to do it himself, he one day filled about 200 cowboys with whiskey intending to get them into trouble with Wild Bill, hoping that they would get to shooting and in the melee shoot the marshal."

Coming upon the pistol-wielding Coe, Hickok drew his own revolver. Some would say that a verbal shootout ensued, with Coe insisting he had fired at a savage stray dog or with the two men recalling their roles on opposite sides of the Civil War. Others would report that Coe then took aim at Hickok and fired two shots, sending a bullet through Hickok's coat, while some would claim that Coe lowered his pistol. It's certain, though, that Hickok pumped two bullets into Coe's stomach.

In the madness of the moment, however, Hickok accidentally shot and killed his friend and special deputy Michael Williams as he ran around the corner of a building to help the marshal. Hickok demanded that the wild bunch of cowboys leave town immediately. Little recorded that Hickok pointed two guns at the drunken lot, asking, "And now do any of you fellow want the rest of these bullets? Get your ponies and ride to your camps or I'll shoot into you."

Hickok then carried his friend's body into the saloon and laid him on a billiard table. He bought a coffin for the man and paid all burial expenses. The accident would haunt him for the rest of his life.

Coe hung on for several days before succumbing to his wounds—the last man known to have died at the hands of Wild Bill Hickok. Coe's body was taken to Brenham, Texas, to be buried near his family at Prairie Lea Cemetery.

Prior to the gun battle at the O.K. Corral, the incident was perhaps the most famous gunfight, representing for folks back East the essence of the Wild West. But in Abilene, controversy erupted over Hickok's actions. Permanent residents there viewed Hickok as a hero, resorting to extreme measures to protect their extremely endangered town. Coe's many cowhand friends, though, believed he was shot without cause. Surrounded by so many potential enemies who might seek vengeance for Coe's death, the gravity of his job weighed on Hickok. He became paranoid, always on guard, avoiding doorways and windows. He was careful to keep a wall behind his back.

Coe's old partner, Ben Thompson, was out of town with his ailing wife when he learned of Coe's death. By the time he returned to Abilene, Hickok had summarily closed down the Bull's Head Saloon.

It would seem that Hickok had few regrets over Coe's death. He supposedly told Welsh journalist and explorer Henry Stanley—who famously tracked down missionary David Livingstone in Africa ("Dr. Livingstone, I presume?")—that he "never killed one man without good cause."

By year's end, Abilene had changed its course and would no longer avail itself to rabble-rousing cattle drivers. The wildest days of Abilene were behind her. Figuring they might now get by with a less costly marshal, and concerned about the questionable shooting of Phil Coe, Abilene parted ways with Hickok in December 1871.

Hickok himself only had five years left to live. While playing cards in Deadwood, Dakota Territory, in 1876, he took a bullet to the back of the head while holding pairs of aces and eights—known to this day as the "dead man's hand."

The Newton Massacre
Deadliest Battle, 1871

The town of Newton, Kansas, just wanted to hold an election. But it would get a bloodbath.

Texas gambler William "Billy" Bailey made his way to the new cattle town of Newton, Kansas, as a cowboy. He was a tough fellow who had killed at least two men. Newton needed someone like him. The city would hold an important election in August to name leaders in the formation of a new county and to make decisions about railroad bonds, and Bailey was asked to deter any political rowdiness. He was appointed as a "Special Policeman."

Bailey wasn't the only one to hold the post. Mike McCluskie, an Irishman from Ohio, had been working for the Santa Fe Railroad as a night watchman and making money on the side as a gambler in Newton. Like Bailey, he was a crusty fellow—earlier in the year, he had been accused of strangling a man to death, though the charges were thrown out. McCluskie was big and powerful, but he was congenial enough—he had taken in James Riley, a local eighteen-year-old dying of tuberculosis. Just the right mix of dangerous and respectable, McCluskie also was appointed as a Special Policeman for Newton to help keep the election madness under control.

Turns out, McCluskie and Bailey didn't care for each other—not at all. They were charged with performing the same job, but a clash of personalities would keep them from their duties.

Cow town Newton's Main Street in 1871, the year of the deadly shootout.
Harvey County Historical Society

On Election Day, August 11, 1871, the two Special Policemen had a bitter argument during the day, apparently over political matters. They disagreed over the ballot and made the very sort of ruckus they were hired to quell.

That night they encountered each other at the Red Front Saloon, just outside town. Their mutual distaste while sober presumably fueled by alcohol into a seething hatred, a fistfight ensued between the men. McCluskie knocked Bailey out the door and into the street and then drew his gun. He fired once, missing, and then again, this time striking Bailey in the chest.

Bailey died the next day, and McCluskie's young friend, Jim Riley, warned him to flee town. Bailey's fellow Texas cowboys surely would be out for revenge, Riley warned. Fearing for his life, McCluskie promptly caught a train to the nearby town of Florence.

He didn't stay gone long enough. McCluskie took a train back to Newton just days later, on August 19. The word on the street was that his shooting of Bailey would be considered self-defense. Although Bailey hadn't drawn his gun, he was a fearsome, lethal figure known to have killed men in previous gunfights. Believing town sentiment was on his side, McCluskie returned. By 10:00 p.m., he was at Tuttle's Dance Hall with a drink in hand.

McCluskie must have enjoyed Newton to have been willing to risk his life in returning. The town was a crazy place on the prairie, full of energy. Newton had been founded in March with the extension of the Santa Fe Railroad and thus the Chisholm Trail, which was used to move steer from Texas to the Kansas railheads. By end of the year, Newton had stolen Abilene's cattle trade and was booming—the town had 1,500 people, ten dance halls, and too many wild cowboys to count. It was a thrilling place for less savory characters such as McCluskie, though more civilized individuals found the town shocking. One wrote of Newton, "Here you may see young girls not over sixteen drinking whisky, smoking cigars, cursing and swearing until one almost looses [sic] the respect they should have for the weaker sex, [sic] I heard one of their townsmen say that he didn't believe there were a dozen virtuous women in town. . . . He further told me if I had any money that I would not be safe with it here. It is a common expression that they have a man every morning for breakfast."

So late on August 19, McCluskie was back in his Kansas town of choice, drinking, gambling, listening to music at Tuttle's Dance Hall with a cowboy friend, Jim Martin, and sickly young companion, Jim Riley, by then known as "McCluskie's Shadow." They might have followed the beaten path to find different music or women at E. P. Crum's Alamo, a dance hall just thirty yards away but returned to Tuttle's place when the Alamo closed just after midnight.

Around that time, dead Billy Bailey's friends were gathering. They moved toward town in a pack, discussing their plans in hushed tones.

Among them was Hugh Anderson, son of a well-to-do rancher in Solado, Texas, but a rough-and-tumble guy nonetheless. Earlier that year he had helped gunfighter John Wesley Hardin track down and kill Juan Bideno in retribution for the murder of Billy Cohron. Now a cowboy in Newton, Anderson had considered Bailey a friend and found himself on another mission of vengeance.

At one in the morning, Perry Tuttle insisted that the place shut down, but customers lingered despite the band's having gone home. At 2:00 a.m. McCluskie was still at his faro table when a handful of Texas cowboys—friends of Billy Bailey— walked in: Anderson's hometown pal Billy Garrett, Henry Kearnes, and Jim Wilkerson.

Then in came Hugh Anderson, leader of the pack. With his pistol drawn, Anderson hollered at McCluskie, "You are a cowardly son-of-a-bitch! I will blow the top of your head off!"

Jim Martin jumped up to stop the fight, but it was too late. McCluskie was falling to the dusty floor, shot in the neck.

The lumbering McCluskie wasn't dead, though. He pulled himself up, pointed his own gun at Anderson, and pulled the trigger.

Misfire. Anderson hit him again, this time in the leg. As McCluskie finally slumped over, Anderson fired another bullet into his back.

Meanwhile, Anderson's pals Garrett, Kearns, and Wilkerson began firing, perhaps to keep the crowd back.

Finally, teenaged Jim Riley drew his pistols and fired toward the assailing Texans. But one of his bullets was intercepted by friend Jim Martin's jugular. The good-natured cowboy known as "Happy Jim Martin" from Refugio, Texas, wobbled out into the night and died on the steps of yet another dance hall.

But Riley got the men he was after. He shot the whole lot of what the *Emporia News* would term "bloodthirsty Texans," striking Anderson in the thigh and leg, Garrett in the shoulder, Kearnes in the chest, and Wilkerson in the nose and leg. He also managed to mow down two innocent bystanders: Hickey, a foreman for the Santa Fe Railroad, was shot in the calf, and railway brakeman Patrick Lee took a slug to the stomach.

Riley, the young local man with tuberculosis who had never before been involved in a gunfight, had struck seven men—killing four of them—in a smoke-filled room with a pair of Colt revolvers. He had exacted revenge on the revenge-seekers (and shot a handful of others). He walked out of Tuttle Dance Hall, his subsequent whereabouts and fate unknown to this day.

McCluskie was carried upstairs. By the time the two town doctors arrived to find a blood-soaked building and wounded men, he was beyond repair. McCluskie died just after sunup, and a dispatch was sent to his mother in St. Louis.

Texas cowboy Wilkerson would survive his grazed nose and wounded leg, but his friends weren't so lucky. Garrett, bleeding from the shoulder and chest, would die later in the day, never to see his hometown of Solado, Texas, again; Kearnes would succumb to his chest wound in a week. As for the innocent bystanders, Hickey survived his leg wound, but Lee died within a couple days.

Hugh Anderson, the leader of the pack of vengeance-seekers, had been struck twice in the leg. A warrant was issued for his arrest, but Marshal Harry Nevill delayed serving the warrant, apparently waiting for Anderson's condition to approve. Most figured the cowboy would soon bleed out anyway.

They were wrong.

Anderson's friends smuggled him out of town onto a train— to Kansas City, perhaps, or Topeka—and he never stood trial for the revenge murder of Mike McCluskie.

The "Newton Massacre," as it would become known, killed five men and wounded three more—making it deadlier than more famous shootouts at the O.K. Corral and Tombstone, Arizona.

According to the *Emporia News*, Newton's government on the night of the massacre was in a pitiful state of affairs.

"Anderson and his men had such control over the crowd that the officers were afraid to arrest them," the paper reported a few days after the event, chastising the town for letting such chaos ensue. "This was one of the bloodiest affrays that ever occurred in our State, and we hope that measures will be taken to prevent its recurrence."

Newspapers across the country described Newton as a cesspool of prostitution, gambling, and excessive drinking. "Pistol shooting is the common amusement," they wrote. In the August 22 issue of Topeka's *Kansas Daily Commonwealth*, one particularly dramatic witness of the events wrote of Newton as though it were a gateway to hell:

While at Newton a few days ago, we were informed
that inasmuch as a man had been killed there on
the morning of the day of our arrival, a week would
probably elapse ere another killing scrape would occur;
that usually after a killing in that town no events of
any moment, saving an occasional head breaking or an
unimportant stabbing affray, occurred for a week or so.
That information was correct for just a week sped by
before a season of bloodshed and slaughter was again
inaugurated. On Sunday (which is the devil's favorite
day for big operation in that town) last, the demon of
discord was again let loose, and riot, blood and murder
was rampant to an unusual degree. It seems as if the
week of respite had sharpened the appetite of the devil
and given him additional vigor and disposition to riot in
a carnival of blood.

Another, this one in the *New York World* on August 21:

The air of Newton is tainted with the hot steam of
human blood. Murder, 'most foul and unnatural,' has
again stained the pages of her short history, and the
brand of Cain has stamped its crimson characters on the
foreheads of men with horrible frequency.

The *Commonwealth* weighed in again on August 23, this
time going so far as to insist that martial law be brought to
Newton. The paper pointed out that Newton had no proper
city government and that the township authorities that did
exist were "inadequate to govern such a lawless and reckless class as predominates in that town." The incident, the
capital's paper said, was "a burning shame and disgrace to
Kansas, and measures should be at once adopted to prevent
a repetition. . . . Let us have no more of such sickening and
shocking tragedies."

While the state and country were fretting over Newton's soul, townspeople set about getting their ducks in a row. There was some division over who deserved blame for the tragedy. Most said the band of cowboys was to blame for instigating the shootout, but their many friends were quick to point out that McCluskie's young friend Riley was the one who did most of the killing. Plus, McCluskie had been well liked around town. As one paper reported, "The deceased was popular among his fellows. Good natured, generous, dangerous only when maddened by liquor, his bad qualities were forgotten and Texas sympathy was oblivious to ought but what endeared him to them."

No matter who was to blame, though, the people of Newton considered their governing troubles more pressing than hunting down Hugh Anderson or Jim Riley. The magistrate said he'd close down the city dance halls—for good. No one vocally objected, but such an ordinance didn't come to pass. Instead a large group of citizens convened to nominate city government candidates for mayor, police judge, marshal, and five city councilmen. Even the numerous Texas cowboys who spent considerable time driving cattle to and from Newton sat in on meetings, agreeing to work with locals to assure order. A police force, including five deputies, was formed. An ordinance banning weapons in Newton was passed. There was talk of raising money for a town hall, church, and schoolhouse. Judge R. W. P. Muse, among the leaders of this reformation, said, "Newton is now to begin afresh." The Newton Massacre, while a tragedy, had successfully shocked the town into cleaning up its act.

No one knows where Hugh Anderson holed up after he was sneaked out of Newton following his murder of Mike

McCluskie. But one thing is for certain: He didn't die of his injuries. In fact, he made it back to Kansas. In summer 1873 he was tending bar at Harding's Trading Post in Medicine Lodge—little more than a smattering of shanties just north of Indian Territory. It was about as obscure a location as a hiding man might find. But someone found him anyway.

Mike McCluskie had a brother, Arthur. Arthur wanted to avenge his brother's death, just as Anderson had avenged Bill Bailey's and Jim Riley had attempted to avenge McCluskie's.

Arthur hired a guide by the name of Richards who tracked down Anderson and delivered a chilling message from the dead McCluskie's brother. Arthur challenged him to a duel, and Anderson could choose the weapon—gun or knife.

Anderson accepted the challenge and chose pistols for weapons; knowing the size of his opponent's brother, he figured Arthur would be a large man, best fought from a distance. Anderson drafted his boss, Harding, to manage the duel. Then he closed down the bar, saying he had "a chore to do."

At dusk, a big crowd gathered on a red-dirt road in Medicine Lodge to watch the duel. Many of them had a good deal of money riding on the outcome.

Anderson and McCluskie regarded each other. Anderson was right—his opponent was a big guy. Then it was time for the show.

The pair stood about twenty paces apart, with their backs turned. Then Harding fired a signal shot and the two men spun to face each other, firing hastily. Their first shots missed, but McCluskie fired again, this time breaking Anderson's arm with a bullet.

Anderson dropped to his knees but managed a shot of his own, striking McCluskie in the mouth. McCluskie, losing blood and teeth, screamed and charged, perhaps thinking of his brother's death.

Anderson kept firing, nailing McCluskie in the leg and stomach, and this time the avenging brother was stopped in his tracks. The duel was over. Anderson had prevailed again. Or so it seemed.

McCluskie looked up, cranked his head toward Anderson and aimed his revolver. Bleeding from his face, leg, and abdomen, he managed to shoot Anderson in the stomach, sending him toppling. Now both men were on the ground. But McCluskie wasn't done yet. He pulled out his knife and crawled painfully through the dirt toward Anderson. By this point the crowd was growing uneasy with the savage scene, but Harding let the bloody duel continue. Anderson, spewing blood from his gut as he watched McCluskie make his way toward him, somehow sat up and drew his own knife. The two men collided on the ground. Anderson hacked into McCluskie's neck; McCluskie stabbed Anderson in the side. Both died there, covered in red blood and red dirt.

The cycle of revenge was finally over and done.

Kate Bender
Femme Fatale, 1872

An Independence, Kansas, man by the name of Wetzell suffered from excruciating neuralgia. Medical remedies being what they were in 1872, Wetzell had little choice but to live in pain. So when he read an advertisement for the supernatural healing powers of a German woman near Cherryvale, he readied his horse and carriage for the fourteen-mile journey across southeast Kansas.

The ad likely read something like this one, which began circulating in the summer of that year:

Prof. Miss KATIE BENDER
Can heal all sorts of Diseases; can cure Blindness, Fits,
Deafness and all such diseases, also Deaf and Dumbness.
Residence, 14 miles East of Independence, on the road
from Independence to Osage Mission one and one half
miles South East of Norahead Station.
Katie Bender
June 18, 1872

It was autumn when Wetzell made his way to see Kate Bender, with his friend Gordan riding along. As the leaves fell around them, Wetzell must have been full of hope—hope to be cured, to live a normal, pain-free existence. Perhaps he was skeptical of the woman's claims, or perhaps he had heard of her work as a medium in the area and was impressed. Either way, he had decided to pay her a visit.

Wetzell and Gordan entered a hollow of cottonwood and plum trees, cut by a shallow stream called Drum Creek. There they found the Bender residence and pulled up near dinnertime. It was a primitive, square structure on the much-traveled road from Fort Scott or Osage Mission to Independence. The place was just eighteen miles from the border of Indian Territory, now the state of Oklahoma. It was sparsely populated frontier, and the Bender family—four German immigrants—had set up an inn for feeding and boarding travelers just over a year prior.

Wetzell and Gordan entered the place to meet John Bender, perhaps sixty years of age, a thin man of average height and few English speaking skills; his wife, around the same age, with blue eyes and brown hair and only slightly better English; John Jr., a mustached young man with a thick accent; and finally Kate, the young daughter with auburn hair and a commanding presence. Kate, with her perfect English and outgoing persona, seemed to be the leader of the small pack.

The inn was a one-room house with a large canvas hung to separate two sections: the front, with shelves of basic groceries for sale and a table for serving meals, and the back, with beds for the family and guests and a trapdoor to a cellar. Behind the house were a garden, an orchard, and a few livestock in a barn.

Kate flashed her pretty dark eyes at the men and insisted that they have dinner before Wetzell's healing session could begin.

As they sat down to eat, the men found that their chairs had been situated snugly and awkwardly against the canvas partition. Then they noticed that the two Bender men, John Sr. and John Jr., were bustling behind the curtain. Something didn't feel right. Nervous, the men insisted on eating while standing up. They moved away from the table, and charming Kate transformed into an angry whirlwind, chastising them for their bad manners.

Wetzell and Gordan quickly left the uncomfortable situation, hopping into their carriage as the Benders stood outside staring and consorting. Two wagons happened by, and the men raced to join them on the road, looking back to see the odd family watching as they went. They didn't notify authorities and went back to Independence, Wetzell still ailing from neuralgia but happy to be out of the Benders' midst.

When the two men finally shared their story, they decided that they had overreacted. What had happened? A family of innkeepers tried to feed them dinner. Nothing more, right? Unbeknownst to them, others would have similar tales from the inn.

William Pickering, a wealthy man from back East, noticed disturbing stains on the canvas partition and hurried away. Father Paul Ponziglione, a middle-aged Catholic missionary who established several churches in the state, rushed out of the house for his horse when he saw John Sr. holding a hammer behind the canvas.

People from all walks of life reported that something wasn't quite right at the Bender Inn.

The Benders had arrived in Labette County in the fall of 1870, when they built their first shanty on the property of country grocer and fellow German immigrant Rudolph Brockmann. By the time they moved on to their modest inn near the Osage Mission Trail, the Benders were known to be a quiet, even strange lot. But Kate was a different story.

Vivacious and outgoing, Kate made appearances at county dances and briefly waited tables at a hotel in Cherryvale. She even went to church on Sunday, spreading the word there that she was deeply in touch with the spiritual world. In fact, she claimed, she was a medium. Kate claimed she could summon and commune with the spirits of dead loved ones—for a price. She began holding séances for locals and found such success that she took her act on the road. During the summer of 1872, Kate toured small Kansas towns such as Parsons, Labette, Oswego, and Chetopa, lecturing on spiritualism in theaters and halls. In those days, it was rare to see a lone woman professing on stage, and her show was a hit. Kate herself was a hit too—for her sharp eyes and dark auburn hair.

By the fall of 1872, when Wetzell and his friend met Kate and her family, the clairvoyance road trip was over. Kate had more important business to tend to at the Bender Inn.

That fall, people started disappearing. Travelers making their way past Cherryvale would go missing, and by March 1873 perhaps a dozen individuals had traveled into the area and never come out. Locals wondered what sort of bad luck was in their midst. Little was done about the situation, though, until a prominent, wealthy doctor was among the missing.

Dr. William York was among the most esteemed citizens of Independence, not far from Cherryvale and the Bender Inn. He had the finest things—a well-bred horse, a quality saddle, luxurious clothes and boots, and an expensive gold watch. And he came from good stock. One of the good doctor's brothers was a state senator and among the most powerful men in the state. Another brother, Col. A. M. York at Fort Scott, was a man of great wealth.

William visited Colonel York in Fort Scott in March 1873, leaving on the ninth of the month to return to Independence. He stayed the night at Osage Mission and, upon leaving there on the tenth, told friends he planned to have lunch at the Bender Inn. He shared the same plans with another friend he met on the road just two miles from the Bender place. Then he disappeared.

Another story about Dr. York goes like this: He lent a horse and buggy to a man and his young daughter, who never returned. Dr. York went looking for them along the Osage Mission Trail and disappeared himself.

The details of his trip might be disputed today, but it's certain that Dr. York was never seen again.

Days passed, then weeks. Colonel York made it his business to find his missing brother, hiring investigators and rounding up search teams. Sniffing around the area, Colonel York happened upon the man named Wetzell, who shared his story of his creepy encounter with the Bender family.

On April 3 a large group rode on horseback to the Bender Inn. The family said they knew nothing of Dr. York. Unconvinced, the colonel returned a few weeks later with a dozen armed locals. By then, though, the Bender family was gone.

The group found starving livestock in the barn and little remaining in the house but a sledgehammer and a knife. It was obvious that the Benders had no plans to return.

Searching the property, the group opened the trapdoor to the pitlike cellar beneath the house. They found the dark hole streaked and splattered with blood.

Fanning across the property, they would find ten bodies buried in the orchard behind the house, as well as another in Drum Creek. One of the victims was Dr. York. All the bodies

The Bender family's many victims, unearthed in 1873, as Labette County residents look on. *Kansas State Historical Society*

had their skulls crushed and their throats slit—all except a small girl, who may have been buried alive. She was identified as the daughter of George Loncher, who was among the slit-throated bodies. The father and daughter had been en route to Iowa after Loncher's wife died.

Investigators surmised that the Benders had run their deadly inn with a consistent strategy. First the guest would be seated for a meal with his back to the canvas room divider. He would be seated so close to the canvas that his head could easily be detected from the other side. While Kate and her mother served the food, one of the Bender men would swing a hammer to crack the victim's skull. The victim's throat then would be slit before his body was robbed of any valuables and dumped through the trapdoor in the floor. Later the body would be buried in the orchard. Because they preyed on people far from home, they had been able to carry on this way for many months before arousing real suspicions.

Once the Benders' serial killing was revealed, posses of vigilantes were formed. Colonel York offered a reward for the capture of his brother's murderers, as did state and local officials. The governor's proclamation of the award, posted throughout the area, described the four Benders, including the "good looking, well formed, rather bold in appearance" Kate. The statement also suggested that John Jr. might actually be one John Gebardt, but the true nature of the four suspects' relationships would never be known.

Vigilantes got hold of Rudolph Brockmann, the German farmer who first met the Benders in Labette County and let them squat on his land. Rumors flew that he and Kate were lovers; surely he knew their whereabouts. The posse strung Brockmann up by a noose, demanding that he divulge any information he had. After several tries at strangling him into submission, the men finally let him go.

Meanwhile the Bender Inn had become a grisly tourist attraction. People came from great distances to see the place, be photographed there, and tear pieces from the structure for souvenirs. Before long the place had been destroyed, but its former occupants remained at large.

Stories about the Benders' escape, or possible demise, filled streets and newspapers across the country.

Some reported that the four had split up at the train station to avoid identification as a group. Other reports had them escaping to Mexico. Or Canada. Or returning to Germany.

Still others suggested that the Benders had run into other criminals and met their demise. Vigilantes had caught the Benders and hanged them, some said. No, they were shot. No, burned to death.

Three years later, a Chicago man claimed to have gotten the real story when he met a Kansas man on a train to Washington Territory.

"During the conversation," the man wrote to the local paper, "knowing that he was from the vicinity of the Bender murders, I expressed my astonishment that these people, ignorant of and unfamiliar with the geography of this country as they must have been, had been so successful in making their escape from the officers of the law, especially as a large reward had been offered for their apprehension. In a half-confidential tone, and in a manner which lent credence to his statement and impressed me with a belief of his honesty, he said that so far as he was concerned there was no mystery about it." According to the report, the Kansas man went on to say that Colonel York's posse indeed had apprehended and killed the Benders.

This theory was thrown for a loop the next year, though, when a man and woman believed to be John Bender Sr. and his wife were arrested in Omaha. Their identity could not be confirmed, and they were released.

Then, in November 1889, two women were arrested in Oswego, Kansas, believed to be Kate and her mother. But their identities were confirmed to be otherwise, and the women finally were released in January 1890.

In 1901 four individuals were apprehended near Fort Collins, Colorado. Again, no dice.

But in 1908 a new development revived the old theory that the Benders had themselves been killed. On his deathbed, former Independence resident George Evans Downer said he had been among a five-man posse who chased the Benders over the prairie on a dark, cloudy night. The Benders fired from their wagon, killing one of the vigilantes, Downer said. The group finally caught up with the family, shooting all but Kate, who jumped from the wagon, cut one of the horses loose and sped off. The posse shot her horse, which fell on Kate, killing her.

But wait! In 1910 a California woman announced that she had been a friend of Kate Bender, now known as Mrs. Peters, and that Kate had died recently of natural causes.

The case continued to fascinate for decades. The minutes from a 1938 Kansas State Historical Society report that the organization received a call asking whether Kate Bender had been captured or killed. And for some years the town of Cherryvale hosted an annual Bender Day celebration, complete with a nineteenth-century costume contest and a living descendant of a Bender victim.

The "bloody Benders" lived on in infamy, but it's still unknown whether they lived on in the flesh. A Kansas state historical marker outside Cherryvale reads, "The end of the Benders is not known. The earth seemed to swallow them, as it had their victims."

Ben Thompson
Dapper and Dangerous, 1873

Ben Thompson had perhaps the most unlikely origins of all the famed gunslingers of the Wild West. He was a Yorkshire man, born in 1842 in Knottingley, England, as the first child of a British naval officer. But the family emigrated to join family in Austin, Texas, when Thompson was nine years old, placing him on a trajectory that would lead to outlaw infamy.

He also had an unlikely appearance, befitting his English roots. Among the dirty cowboys, wearing chaps and broken-down boots in the Kansas and Texas towns Thompson inhabited, he dressed sharply, preferring an elegant frock coat over a vest and cravat, complete with a stovetop hat and a cane. But underneath the well-kept exterior was an ill-kept temper. Once out-of-town ruffians mistook him for a New England "dandy," taunting him and knocking off his hat. He responded by opening fire, hitting one of the fleeing men in the ear and the side.

Thompson spent his adolescence in Austin, attending school into his teens and then working for two years as a printer for a city newspaper. In 1860, at the age of eighteen, he moved to New Orleans and found work as a bookbinder. It was respectable work, but soon his fiery personality got the best of him. He had to leave town after getting into a knife fight.

The Civil War found Thompson serving in the Confederate army in Col. John Ford's 2nd Texas Cavalry. He was wounded in the battle of Galveston Bay and fought a losing battle at LaFourche Crossing in Louisiana.

While on furlough in 1863—not for battle wounds but rather for a whiskey-smuggling incident during which his horse fell on him—he married Catherine Moore, daughter of an affluent Austin merchant. But he returned to the warfront, until he killed a man in an argument over an army mule. Federal soldiers hauled him in, and he sat in an Austin jail awaiting trial.

Nothing could keep Thompson tied down for long, though. He bribed two guards to get him out of town and fled to Mexico. He remained south of the border for two years, fighting in Emperor Maximilian's army until the fall of the empire in 1867 and also finding time to kill a Mexican police officer who came after him with a knife, reportedly over Thompson's flirtations with a woman.

In 1868 Thompson was back in Austin—and back in trouble. His brother-in-law, James Moore, had been a thorn in his side since he sold Thompson's mother's iron cookware to a cannon factory during the war. Now Moore was beating his sister—Thompson's wife. Thompson shot Moore in the side and later, standing before the court, threatened to kill the judge. This time there would be no rinky-dink town jail and malleable guards. Thompson was sentenced to hard time—four years of labor in the Texas State Penitentiary at Huntsville. He served two years of the sentence before being pardoned by President Ulysses S. Grant.

After so many run-ins with the law, Thompson needed to get out of Texas and stay out. He heard that a Kansas town called Abilene was coming into a boom along a cattle trail from Texas. Thompson and his wife moved there in 1870.

Ben Thompson as marshal of Austin, Texas, following his saloon-running years in Kansas. *Kansas State Historical Society*

At the age of twenty-eight, Thompson already had lived many lives: the British child of a respected naval officer, a Texas teenager working for newspapers and bookbinders, a Confederate soldier, a fighter in the Mexican army, and a penitentiary inmate. He was ready to settle down, earn a decent living, and spend time with his wife and son.

In 1871 Thompson opened the Bull's Head Saloon. Gunman Phil Coe, whom Thompson reportedly had met while serving under Maximilian, joined as a partner, and before long the two were rolling in money. The Bull's Head was a favorite watering hole of the rabble-rousing Texas cowboys who rolled through town with herds of longhorns.

The Bull's Head was the center of much of Abilene's lawlessness, and it drew ire from Abilene's marshal, Wild Bill Hickok. As Thompson's business partner, Coe wasn't much help, provoking Hickok and developing a personal vendetta against the lawman. Thompson left town and his unruly saloon for a time to escape the escalating tensions there. But he, his wife, and son were involved in a serious buggy accident in Kansas City that required his wife's arm to be amputated. During Thompson's lengthy absence from the Bull's Head while at his wife's side, Coe picked a fight with Hickok and wound up dead. The Bull's Head was seized by Hickok and other authorities, and Thompson had nothing to which he might return in Abilene.

Disenchanted with Abilene, in 1873 Thompson moved his family to Ellsworth, Kansas, another boomtown on the cattle trail. There he frequented Joe Brennan's saloon, where he was adept at the card tables.

One day Thompson was running a game of monte at Brennan's and had a few side bets with gambler John Sterling for good measure. Thompson and Sterling had arranged to share any winnings, but his veins full of liquor and his pockets stuffed with money, Sterling left the saloon without paying up.

That afternoon, Thompson found Sterling at another saloon sharing a drink with a law officer known as Happy Jack Morco. Thompson confronted Sterling, who then punched him in the face. Morco drew his gun, so Thompson—unarmed, for a change, in compliance with city ordinance—retreated to Brennan's saloon.

Soon Sterling and Morco burst through the door and challenged Thompson and his friends to a gunfight. Thompson ran to retrieve his rifle and pistol. He was joined by his younger brother, Billy, who was extremely drunk and wielding a shotgun.

Before they reached their opponents, Billy managed to shoot two local law officials, prompting Ben to seize his brother's weapon and hand it to a bystander. Then the elder Thompson yelled for Sterling and Morco to come out and finish what they had started.

Before a fight ensued, Sheriff Chauncey Whitney and former officer John DeLong tried to calm the Thompson brothers. Whitney was a good friend of Billy, who by now had gotten hold of his shotgun again. Whitney suggested that they all sit down and have a quiet drink to calm their nerves.

But it was too late for intervention. Someone on the street yelled a warning to Ben, who turned and saw Sterling and Morco storming his way, weapons drawn. Ben fired his rifle at Morco, who ducked into a doorway and evaded the bullet. Then, in the madness of the moment, Billy somehow managed to shoot and kill his friend Whitney.

Ben was appalled at his brother's drunken actions and sent him out of town. He then holed himself up in a hotel room with his guns. Morco, meanwhile, filed assault charges against him for firing a shot in his direction.

Who would have the guts to pull Thompson from his room? Not even the local police would attempt so dangerous a feat. The mayor himself, James Miller, finally ordered him to give up his weapons, but Thompson wouldn't budge. Disgusted, Miller threw up his hands and fired the entire Ellsworth city police force. County Deputy Sheriff Ed Hogue finally came to the rescue, taking Thompson into custody. He had little to fear from the law, anyway—the next morning, Morco and Sterling failed to show up in court, and Thompson was set free. His troublemaker brother Billy also lucked out. In 1876 he was hauled back to Ellsworth to be tried for Whitney's death, but the murder was ruled an accident and Billy was acquitted.

After their hard times in Kansas, Thompson and his family returned to Austin. Of course with Thompson, trouble was sure to follow. In 1876 he shot Mark Wilson, owner of the Capital Theatre, but was acquitted on the basis of self-defense.

Never one to stay down for long, four years later Thompson was running the Iron Front Saloon on Congress Avenue and serving as the town marshal. Thompson relished the role, drawing attention with his fine duds and commanding authority with his shiny six-shooter. But his time on the right side of the law was to be short-lived. After just two years wearing the badge, during a visit to San Antonio he shot and killed Jack Harris, owner of the Vaudeville Theatre, over a gambling dispute. Thompson resigned as marshal.

That shooting would result not just in the end of his law career but also the end of his life.

In 1884 Thompson shared drinks with King Fisher, deputy sheriff of Uvalde, and unwisely boarded a train to see a play in San Antonio—at the Vaudeville Theatre, where he had killed Jack Harris. After the show, Harris's old friends joined Thompson and Fisher for a tense round of drinks, and confrontational words were exchanged. Finally Thompson slapped one of the men and shoved a gun into his mouth. In the ensuing scuffle, two San Antonio men were wounded—one would die later following a related leg amputation—and both Fisher and Thompson lay dead and riddled with bullet holes.

Billy Brooks
From Crime Fighter to Criminal, 1874

Billy Brooks had a long fall, from the high honor of a marshal's badge to the bottom of a length of rope.

William L. Brooks first made a living as a stagecoach driver working out of El Dorado in Butler County. In his early twenties he relocated to Newton, where his personal grit soon earned him a job as the first town marshal. Brooks was regarded as a mean fellow, and the people of Newton trusted him to scare off criminals. And he surely could have—if not for a habit of getting into trouble himself.

On June 9, 1872, just months after taking the marshal's badge in Newton, Brooks was wounded in the line of duty and celebrated as a hero. The dustup involved a group of Texas cattle drovers who, according to one newspaper, "had corralled the proprietor of a dance-house with their six-shooters, and were carrying things on a high hand." Marshal Brooks, who reportedly had run this bunch out of town once before, entered the dance house to intervene. A shootout ensued, and Marshal Brooks was struck three times—once near the collarbone and twice in the arm.

According to Brooks's sworn deposition before Justice of the Peace George Haliday in the Harvey County district court, two of the unruly cowboys fired at him first. Brooks survived his wounds, having "sand enough to beat the hour-glass that tries to run him out," one local rag stated, and was said to have

Bad cop Billy Brooks, Newton's first marshal. *Kansas State Historical Society*

chased the no-good criminals for ten miles before returning to town for medical attention.

But the cowboys—including James Hunt and E. T. "Red" Beard, who would go on to run a brothel in Wichita—had another story. They insisted that Brooks had tried to kill them. Respectable witnesses must have corroborated, as Brooks found himself in hot water for allegedly abusing his position. A preliminary examination was scheduled for June 10, but prosecutors needed more time to collect evidence against Brooks; the trial was postponed until the next day. In the meantime, Brooks unsuccessfully insisted on a change of venue. The proceedings' outcome is unclear, but Brooks wasn't long for Newton, Kansas.

Brooks moved on to a brief police stint in Ellsworth, but by year's end he was in Dodge City. He worked there as a buffalo hunter, riding out into the prairie to shoot and skin the already dwindling herds of bison.

By now, Brooks's temperament was no secret. Folks around Dodge called him "Bully" Brooks, a nickname he proved to deserve just around Christmastime.

First, on December 23, while the cow town was buzzing with holiday cheer, Brooks encountered an old associate by the name of Brown, who worked as a yardmaster for the Santa Fe Railroad in Newton. There was bad blood between them, and a gunfight erupted. According to witness T. E. Clark, interviewed by the *Wichita Eagle*, each man fired three rounds. Brown managed to wound Brooks with his first shot, but Brooks killed the man with his third—and wounded Brown's friend to boot. "Brooks is a desperate character, and has before, in desperate encounters, killed his man," the paper said.

Five days later, on December 28, Matt Sullivan was working in a Dodge City saloon when a bullet came through the window, killing Sullivan almost instantly. Several people witnessed the event, and though the murderer couldn't be named for certain, suspicion fell squarely on "Bully" Brooks—currently the loosest cannon in town (which, in Dodge, was saying something).

Brooks managed to stay out of trouble through the first of the year, but he'd made plenty of enemies in the area. On March 4, 1873, a beautiful day with a hint of spring in the air, a fellow buffalo hunter named Kirk Jordan fired shots at Brooks with his buffalo gun. According to the diary of yet another buffalo hunter, Henry H. Raymond, the bullet missed Brooks and whizzed through two water barrels. But rumors that Brooks was dead flew quickly—so quickly it seemed people wished it were true.

Brooks finally got out of Dodge. By the summer of 1873 he had set up a new home at Bluff Creek, south of Caldwell, with his wife.

Caldwell was located on the Chisholm Trail, a major cattle-driving route from Texas to Kansas railroad connections that would send livestock to urban areas back East. Countless cowboys and Texas longhorns made their way north through Caldwell to Abilene or Wichita. The place was just a couple miles from the southern Kansas border, beyond which was Indian Territory, present-day Oklahoma. Indian Territory was a wild, lawless place that often served as a refuge for outlaws, and Caldwell's proximity lent an element of danger to the town. Native Americans, themselves under siege, were known to cross the border and attack white settlers. And white horse thieves or other troublemakers could strike and return to Indian Territory in the blink of an eye, with the added bonus that their crimes likely would be deemed an "Indian raid."

Caldwell was a wild place, yes, but it was an increasingly important part of the cattle trade and took measures to secure its own growth. Communications were of particular import, and in the summer of 1874 a private contract for mail delivery was up for grabs. The winning bidder would provide a mail line from Caldwell to nearby towns. Vail and Company beat Southwestern Stage Line for the job, and they were to begin delivery on July 1.

In late June the newspaper of nearby Wellington excitedly reported that Vail and Company workers had passed through with fourteen mules and five small buggies. Soon the delivery route would be up and running, including stops in Wellington, Chetopa, and even Indian Territory.

Well, not if Southwestern Stage Line had anything to say about it.

The disgruntled company, having lost a major payday to Vail and Company, figured it could still cash in on the fledgling mail routes—if Vail and Company failed. But Southwestern wasn't about to sit around waiting for that to happen. Instead they paid a good deal of money to a bevy of thieves, whose job was to steal Vail and Company's mules and horses. Without the animal to pull the mail, the routes would fail and Southwestern would be sure to save the day.

One by one, mules and horses began disappearing from stables. Some belonged to area residents, but most were the property of Vail and Company. On June 29 a particularly bold act resulted in the disappearance of four Vail and Company mules and a horse from Judd Calkins' livery barn in Caldwell.

The horse's owner, A. E. Fletcher, was asleep in the barn when the thieves struck.

July 1, the projected start date for mail delivery, came and went. Almost all of Vail and Company's animals had vanished. In an attempt to fight back, Vail put up a $300 reward for either catching the robbers or bringing in the mules and horses.

The search for the thieves was on.

A. C. "Mack" McLean ran the Last Chance saloon south of Caldwell. All sorts of characters passed through his business, and they tended to talk when they drank too much. McLean had heard a lot of stories from behind the bar, from boasts to exaggerations to outright lies. But one story overheard that July struck him as particularly important.

The group of men drinking whisky at the bar had been rounding up mules. Stealing them. The next morning they would head west with their bounty, to Larned or perhaps Fort Dodge.

McLean confided in Caldwell doctor and druggist P. J. M. Burkett. The thieves would pass the H. J. Devore farm a couple miles west of town around 9:00 a.m. the next morning. McLean, himself a less-than-upright citizen, figured the information would be more credible coming from Burkett. Plus, he was afraid for his own life.

Burkett relayed the information to town leader A. M. Colson, who promptly went about organizing a posse of armed men to catch the bandits. Colson went north of town to the Chikaskia River, where settlers had been hit hard by thieves. He knew he'd find angry men there. Colson also asked Sheriff John G. Davis of Wellington for help. The next morning, a large group of men converged and headed west to the Devore ranch.

But the thieves had moved more quickly than predicted. They'd already passed the area. The vigilantes filled up on breakfast at the Devore place and set out northwest along the Ellsworth Trail. The hunt took much longer than planned, and they didn't have adequate provisions. After a few days, the group was down to nine: Colson, W. B. King, Frank Barrington, Alex Williamson, and John Williams from Caldwell, plus Sheriff Davis, Joe Thralls, John Botkin, and Neal Gatliff from Wellington.

The search carried on in the direction of Fort Dodge. When the posse lost the thieves' trail, the men divided up to look for clues. Luckily they happened upon a boy who had seen the band at Sand Creek, fifteen miles west. There the posse found more tracks and were on the trail again by morning. But, for all the excitement of the new development, the men and their horses had traversed many miles in a matter of days and were ready for the adventure to end.

Finally, near Garfield, there they were—the thieves, a wagon, mules, and horses. The angry mob raced toward them, but the bandits raced off on their horses. Still, a half dozen mules and a couple horses were returned to Vail and Company on July 26, and the men got their $300 reward.

By now the faces of the criminals at large were coming into focus. Saloonkeeper McLean had given a few names, and the vigilantes had laid eyes on a few familiar faces.

One of those faces was William "Bully" Brooks.

The former marshal's fellow thieves made a motley crew. Judson H. "Judd" Calkins ran the City Hotel and owned a Caldwell livery barn that often boarded horses belonging to criminals. Dave P. Terrill was a former owner of the Last

Chance saloon. Sewell Ford, missing a limb and thus known as "One-Armed Charlie," supposedly was the son of a powerful Illinois politician. He also was a notorious drunk who had spent the previous months mooning in front of Caldwell saloons in a dirty brown suit and long, unkempt hair. Mack McLean's name also was on the list, as he consorted with these men, and his informant status was as yet unknown.

Then there was L. Ben Hasbrouck, a dashing, well-to-do young man schooled in New York City and Caldwell's first attorney. Despite his charms, Hasbrouck was known to run with a bad crowd and drink whisky at Last Chance. The previous winter he had been charged with stealing a cow but had successfully argued for his own acquittal. Many residents still held a grudge against him.

Justice of the Peace James A. Dillar put out a warrant for the men, several of whom reportedly had returned to town. Sheriff Davis assembled yet another posse. He left Wellington and waited outside Caldwell in the early-morning hours of July 28. This time, nearly two hundred men showed up.

With darkness on their side, the vigilantes rooted out the thieves, one by one. Judd Calkins gave himself up without a fight at the City Hotel. The handsome Hasbrouck was found hiding in a field. Dave Terrill was driven out of a friend's home three miles northwest of Caldwell. A. C. McLean, the secret informant, was dragged from his place south of town. One-Armed Charlie caught wind of the raid and made haste for Indian Territory, but about fifteen men tailed him for miles on horseback, finally capturing him. Billy Brooks, caught sleeping in his home near Bluff Creek, was intent on going down fighting. Two men exited the house, handed over their guns, and were released. But Brooks shouted to Sheriff Davis that he and his wife had no plans to come out.

According to a Caldwell minister's wife, who heard a first-hand account, their exchange was long and dramatic.

"Come out and give yourself up like a man," Sheriff Davis yelled.

"You'll never take me alive," Brooks replied.

The sheriff implored that he would protect Brooks from the mob and that he would see to a just courtroom proceeding. Brooks wasn't buying it.

"I'll never get to Wellington alive," he said.

"I have control of my men, and if you give yourself up, I pledge my word you'll have a fair trial," Sheriff Davis insisted.

"I know the mob will hang me, and I will not give myself up alive. If you take me, you'll take me a dead man."

Davis demanded that Brooks at least send out his wife, a small, pale woman with curly hair and large eyes.

"My wife will not leave," Brooks said, claiming that his delicate wife was ready for battle. "She is a better warrior than you or any of the men you have in your crowd."

"I have two hundred men, and it will not take long to bring you out," Davis threatened, but Brooks' bravado was interminable.

"I'm all ready, so go right ahead without any more talk," he taunted.

In the end, it was all for show. Brooks finally relinquished himself to the sheriff's mob and, as promised, made it to town alive. He and the other prisoners found themselves in the Wellington jail. Terrill was released, apparently deemed innocent, and businessman Calkins posted $500 bail. McLean also was released, as the town doctor let it be known that he'd simply overheard the thieves at Last Chance.

By Wednesday, July 29, only three of the original suspects remained in jail. Attorney William Hackney, a friend of the released men and a future state representative, insisted that Terrill, Calkins, and McLean were guilty of nothing more than keeping bad company. Afraid they'd be hanged, Hackney had made sure they got out of jail. Arrest warrants were reissued for Calkins and Terrill—but they were long gone, having hired a team of horses to escape to Wichita. After the circus surrounding the men's capture, the people of Caldwell were angry that potential horse thieves had been set free. No matter that Brooks, Hasbrouck, and Ford would stand before a judge the next morning. They were ready to take matters into their own hands.

"Considerable excitement prevailed, and grave fears that an attempt would be made to lynch the prisoners was entertained by not a few," one newspaper reported.

Sensing the makings of a dangerous mob, a Presbyterian minister from Caldwell rode to Wellington. As the sun was setting, he asked to visit with the three remaining captives. Sheriff Davis turned him away, telling him to come back in the morning. Soon the minister found himself locked inside the home of a friend. No man of God was to meddle that night.

It was about midnight when the large pack of men, carrying guns and riding horses, took over the Wellington jail. The guards on duty could do little to stop the mob. Soon the prisoners, including Billy Brooks, were being marched under a big, bright moon to Slate Creek Bridge. There, at a nearby oak tree, the mob threw ropes over a high, sturdy limb and hanged all three of them.

The Wellington newspaper headline shouted "DEAD! DEAD!! DEAD!!!" and went on to describe the "ghastly spectacle" of such a "fearful retribution."

The bodies, witnessed by many, were hanged from the same branch. Brooks' face was distorted, indicating "a horrible struggle with death," though Hasbrouck and Ford "looked naturally, and evidently died easily." It was a sensational lynching: a former lawman, a member of the Sumner County bar, and a one-armed drunk.

Brooks's wife came to town from Caldwell, some said by foot, to find her husband's body stretched out with his partners in the Sumner County courthouse. But there would be no prosecuting any members of the murderous mob of vigilantes. Instead Mack McLean—the saloonkeeper who had assisted in the hunt and then been arrested himself—ended up standing trial on August 5. During the proceedings, more details of the thievery came to light, adding gloom to an already bleak day, during which droves of grasshoppers decimated area crops.

Dr. Burkett defended his informant, and an area rancher confirmed that McLean had no part in the thefts.

Burr Mosier had kept a ranch near Buffalo Creek, one mile south of Caldwell, for about a year. He testified that around July 1, Jasper Marion, also known as Granger, stopped by Burr's ranch "for grub." Over his meal, Granger blabbed to Mosier that he was in possession of eight mules that belonged to Vail and Company, not to mention a horse stolen by mistake and belonging to A. E. Fletcher. Granger rattled off more details, including the names of men involved: Hasbrouck, Ford, and of course Brooks. He also named Jerry Williams, Henry Hall, and three men known only as Red, Jim, and Bob, for a total of nine thieves including Granger. Granger went on to say that the stolen mules were stashed just five miles away at Turkey Creek.

Indeed, Mosier testified, he saw the mules at that location less than a week later, by this time numbering ten. He saw Brooks and Granger there too.

According to Mosier, Granger and Brooks planned to ride to the town of Kingfisher, where they would empty a stable of Vail and Company's last mules. Meanwhile, One-Armed Charlie would steal what he could at Stinking Creek. The Kingfisher group failed its mission—in fact, Granger's horse was shot and a fellow thief killed and scalped by Indians before they reached the Vail and Company horses. The other group fared better.

The next day, Burr testified, Billy Brooks blew through his ranch in a Southwestern company coach. Two of Vail and Company's mail drivers had delivered U.S. mail to Burr just moments earlier, riding in a sulky pulled by a single horse— perhaps the company's last steed. Brooks and his companion planned to follow them and seize that horse too. But, afraid of another Indian attack, they commissioned Burr to join them with his own gun. Brooks told Burr to charge his services to Southwestern Stage, which would pay any expense to stop the transmission of mail from Caldwell to Fort Sill. Brooks and his fellow outlaws already had earned $600.

Burr's testimony ran in the local paper with the headline "Truth Stranger Than Fiction." McLean was acquitted of any involvement in the scheme. Of the nine men who were involved in stealing the livestock and crippling Vail and Company's mail route, none would see trial. And three, including "Bully" Brooks, would never see another day.

Dirty Dave Rudabaugh
Scent of an Outlaw, 1876

In a time when baths were few and far between—and a place where personal hygiene was considerably compromised—and among men whose teeth were as yellow as the sun, Dave Rudabaugh *still* managed to earn a reputation for being dirty. His grimy, disheveled appearance—and signature odor—somehow offended even gunslingers of the West in the late 1800s.

"Dirty Dave" Rudabaugh was born in Fulton County, Illinois, in 1854. His father died in the Civil War when Rudabaugh was a child, and the young boy and his destitute family bounced around between Illinois and Ohio. They finally settled in Eureka, Kansas, where Rudabaugh spent his adolescence before leaving home in his teens in the early 1870s.

As so many would-be outlaws were wont to do, Rudabaugh spent his younger years drifting from job to job, tiring quickly of positions as a bartender, messenger, cowboy, and ranch manager. It's not as though there wasn't excitement in these lines of work. Bartenders saw the wild nights of the frontier's saloons; messengers needed vigilance against bandits and Indians during their travels; cowboys enjoyed a rugged freedom and plenty of whiskey. While working for the well-respected Charlie Rath moving buffalo hides from bustling Dodge City to Adobe Walls, a Texas trading outpost, Rudabaugh barely missed a bloody attack by Kiowa, Comanche, and Arapaho Indians.

Indeed, there was plenty of excitement to be found in respectable work. But Rudabaugh wasn't long in these sorts of jobs, perhaps because the money was too slow, or perhaps because his fellow workers couldn't tolerate his stench. By the early 1870s, when he was still a teenager, Dirty Dave Rudabaugh had found his true calling: outlaw.

Just as Rudabaugh somehow out-stank the stinkiest cowboys on the trail, he would gain a reputation as a particularly vile character among renegades. Whether holding up stages in the Black Hills of South Dakota or rustling cattle along the western border of Arkansas, Rudabaugh was notably ruthless and wore a permanent scowl. His dark eyebrows were always furrowed over his small eyes, and his thick, handlebar mustache seemed to elongate his frown. His rumpled, sweat-stained clothing and rancid breath were the perfect complement to Rudabaugh's foul demeanor. A dangerous and ruthless bully, he looked out only for himself—an approach that served him well through his early years of lawbreaking.

But any outlaw could use a couple partners in crime. When Rudabaugh landed in Dodge City in 1876, he put together a cattle-rustling group that might maximize his profits. The group, called "the Trio," included Rudabaugh, Mike Roarke, and Dan Dement and terrorized area cowboys, plucking valuable livestock from their herds.

By November 1877, a few more gunfighters had joined the Trio, rendering its name defunct. The pack, then known as the Rudabaugh-Roarke Gang, was now big enough to make a major haul.

But Rudabaugh picked the wrong robbery when he and his gang stole valuables from a Santa Fe Railroad construction site near Dodge City in late 1877. Mayor Dog Kelley and the railroad banded together to catch the criminals, commandeering Wyatt Earp as a U.S. deputy marshal. Earp would earn a whopping $10 a day plus room and board to hunt down Dirty Dave. Earp tracked him four hundred miles south to Fort Griffin, Texas—a wild town full of ne'er-do-wells—but Rudabaugh had already come and gone.

Luckily, at Shanssey's Saloon Earp found a gambler with a rattling cough who remembered the stinky, mustached grouch. The gambler's name was Doc Holliday, and it seemed he had made a trade of sorts with the outlaw: Dirty Dave's gun tips for Doc's card tricks. Holliday had managed to gather from Rudabaugh that he was headed back to Kansas, perhaps by way of West Texas. Earp wired the tip back to Dodge City.

1878 sketch of cowboys herding valuable Texas steer—coveted by cattle rustlers like Rudabaugh—into Dodge City. *Kansas State Historical Society*

Indeed, Rudabaugh had doubled back on his trail and returned to Kansas in the dead of winter. Reunited with his gang, Rudabaugh pitched the idea of robbing a Santa Fe train in the heart of Dodge City. His partner Roarke, though, insisted this would be a suicide mission, as the place was teeming with officers already on the lookout for them. So they settled on another spot, not so far away. In late January, in the dark hours of a cold morning, Rudabaugh and four of his gang struck a train in the town of Kinsley and hightailed north. This "safe" robbery didn't turn out to be so safe, nor did it turn out to be a robbery. The gang failed to secure any valuables, and a posse of lawmen from Dodge nabbed Rudabaugh. The men tried to pry from him the names of his accomplices.

It didn't take much prying. Rudabaugh happily reported the names of his "friends" in exchange for his own freedom. The four men were brought in and imprisoned based on Rudabaugh's testimony, and Rudabaugh was let loose.

Rudabaugh, along with the Kansas cohorts he hadn't sold down the river, made his way to Las Vegas in New Mexico Territory in early 1879. His "Dodge City Gang" included famous outlaw "Mysterious Dave" Mather and John Joshua Webb, a former city marshal who had hunted Rudabaugh back in Kansas. The men—all thieves, murderers, and bandits—declared themselves law officials and took over Las Vegas. But they had a curious way of policing the town. They took what they pleased from common folk and killed any man who crossed them; they lynched the three men who killed one of their gang, Joe Carson; and they robbed two stages and a train in the area by year's end. The October train robbery scored them more than $2,000 and a handful of weapons, not to mention all the train's lanterns (a handy commodity at the time).

The next spring, former Dodge City marshal Webb found himself facing the noose for murdering an area rancher, Michael Helliher. Webb had spent more than a month in a Las Vegas jail when in late April he heard someone come crashing into the jail. A gun fired, and the deputy sheriff on guard was dead. Dave Rudabaugh and an associate, Little Jack Allen, were attempting to bust Webb from jail. Other officials made it to the scene, however, and Webb's escape failed.

Rudabaugh's and the Dodge City Gang's run of Las Vegas was coming to an end—they had far too much blood on their hands to avoid vigilante lynch mobs. Rudabaugh, Allen, and another partner headed south out of town. Allen didn't make it far, though—Rudabaugh shot and killed him, in case he might say a word about the jail guard's death.

Rudabaugh found ranch work near Fort Sumner in New Mexico Territory. There a fellow ranch hand introduced him to a curious fellow called Billy the Kid. Billy's gang, the Rustlers, was just the kind of night job Rudabaugh was looking for. He joined them in plundering New Mexico Territory and the Texas panhandle. Rudabaugh quickly emerged as the nastiest of the lot, and even Billy the Kid—among the wildest, craziest men of his day—felt uneasy around the foul-smelling Dodge City bully.

In late November 1880 Rudabaugh and his new clan, the Rustlers, ran into a deputy in the small town of White Oaks. Shots were fired, but the Rustlers made it to a nearby ranch and took cover, holding the owner hostage. When the sun rose the next day, a posse managed to free the rancher, but a new gunfight erupted and a deputy sheriff lay dead. The Rustlers escaped.

They went undetected for a month, but a ride into Fort Sumner at Christmastime would mean more bloodshed, this time among the Rustlers. A posse sprang from an old hospital building and besieged the group of riders. The ensuing gun battle took down Rudabaugh's horse, and Rudabaugh hopped onto a fellow Rustler's steed. The outlaws made it to a cabin near Stinking Springs—an aptly named hideout for Dirty Dave—and hid there several days until they were discovered once more. This time the posse meant business, gunning down two of the Rustlers and capturing four more—including Rudabaugh and Billy the Kid.

When the shackled outlaws arrived in Las Vegas, a mob was waiting for Dirty Dave Rudabaugh. They hadn't forgotten his killing of the jail guard, and they wanted retribution. He evaded hanging, though, as the officials who captured him were bent on seeing him tried for an assortment of crimes. First, in February 1881 Rudabaugh was convicted of robbing stages—including a U.S. mail stagecoach—in Santa Fe. The sentence: ninety-nine years in the clink. He had pleaded guilty to the robberies, hoping the move would save his life. But the law wasn't done. Rudabaugh finally faced charges for murdering the innocent Las Vegas jail watchman. This sentence rendered the previous one moot; he was scheduled to hang.

In the interim Rudabaugh found himself in jail with Webb, the former marshal he'd tried to spring free. With his life on the line, Rudabaugh was more successful at getting *himself* out of jail. His first attempt resulted in nothing more than the accidental killing of a fellow inmate. The next try was a much quieter one, involving Rudabaugh and Webb chipping a hole in the jail wall. In the fall of 1881 they wiggled out and disappeared in separate directions.

Some say Rudabaugh escaped to Arizona, where he may have ridden into Tombstone just in time for the shootout between the Clanton Gang and Wyatt Earp, Earp's brothers, and Doc Holliday. He did manage to stay low and keep his head for the next few years.

Rudabaugh was a marked man, but he thought he would find a safe haven south of the border, where no one knew his name. In the mid-1880s he was doing ranch work in Mexico, but it didn't take long for his true character to emerge. He was sent packing when his boss caught him stealing cattle.

Rudabaugh found his way to Parral, a silver town complete with brothels, cantinas, and gambling tables, in Chihuahua, Mexico. There he made a living with his deck of cards. Once again, though, where Rudabaugh went, trouble followed. He gained a quick reputation as the scourge of Parral, cheating at cards when he pleased and waving his gun in everyone's face. The people of Parral quickly tired of him.

In February 1886 an outraged local accused Rudabaugh of cheating during a game of cards. Rudabaugh simply replied by shooting the man between the eyes at close range. When cantina patrons drew their guns, Rudabaugh shot one in the arm and another through the heart. He then headed outside toward his horse.

But there was no horse to be found. Somehow, certainly by design, the horse was missing—Rudabaugh had no means for a hasty retreat from his crimes.

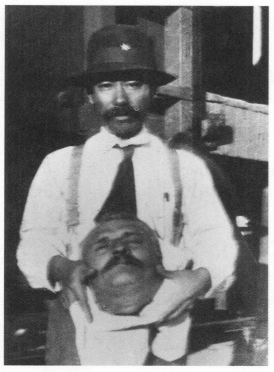

Dirty Dave Rudabaugh's head.
Western History Collections, University of Oklahoma Libraries, Oklahoma Collection 544

Enraged, Rudabaugh stomped back into the cantina with his gun drawn. This time, he wouldn't stomp back out. The people of Parral unloaded their weapons from the shadowy corners of the dark watering hole, killing the man who had tormented their town—along with Dodge City, Las Vegas, and a host of ranchers, cattle drivers, and stage drivers in between. Their disdain for the grimy American was so great that they cut off Rudabaugh's head, mounted it on the end of a long pole, and paraded it about town for all to see. They even took pictures of the severed head, as though to prove to themselves that no one would need fear Dirty Dave Rudabaugh again.

Big Nose Kate
Doc Holliday's Girl, 1878

"Big Nose" Kate Elder felt more at home in scandalous watering holes filled with drunken, stinking renegades than she did in any kitchen or sewing room. She spent much of her life carousing in the most notorious saloons of the Wild West, places where ladies weren't welcome.

But Kate Elder was no lady. She had dark hair and a long, confident face, with prominent cheekbones and a frequent smirk. While other women were wearing aprons over their dresses, Kate was wearing a gun under hers. It was handy protection in her profession of choice—prostitution.

Known as Big Nose Kate to the cowboys and gunslingers looking for a good time, her true identity was much nobler. Born Mary Katherine Haroney in 1850 in Budapest, Hungary, she had a luxurious childhood as the eldest of seven siblings in the home of her wealthy parents, Dr. Michael Haroney and his second wife, Katharina Baldizar. Kate received a fine education and learned to speak Hungarian, French, Spanish, and English. Her father served as a medical doctor for local aristocrats and, when Kate was twelve years old, was named the personal physician for Hapsburg archduke and Mexican emperor Maximilian. The family moved to Mexico City to serve the royal court until Maximilian's regime fell three years later. Amid political upheaval and Maximilian's execution, the Haroneys fled north and settled in Davenport, Iowa.

Prior to her family's flight from Mexico, Kate had enjoyed an easy life. But everything changed that first year in the United States when both her mother and father died within a matter of months. Kate was separated from her siblings in foster care, eventually ending up in the home of a man named Otto Smith. It's believed that the man abused her, as Kate ran away and secretly hopped a steamboat to St. Louis. Along the way, the teenager was discovered by the steamboat captain, a man named Fisher, who helped her establish a life and education in St. Louis. Following her graduation from Catholic school, Kate married a dentist, Silas Melvin, and had a baby. Both husband and infant died in a matter of months, however, echoing the sequential deaths of her parents.

Kate, devastated by her unthinkable losses, needed something to cure the deep sadness she felt. For that she turned to alcohol. She also needed a way to provide for herself, a young widow with no parents. For that she turned to prostitution.

By 1874 Kate had made her way to Kansas and discovered Dodge City. The exciting, alcohol-soaked life to be found there was just what Kate needed to keep her spirits up and her mind off the past. Operating under the memorable name of Big Nose Kate Elder, she worked in a dance hall that may have been owned by Nellie Earp, lawman Wyatt Earp's sister-in-law.

Texas cowboys enjoying a night of revelry after driving a large herd of longhorns hundreds of miles, respectable lawmen having a drink and keeping an eye on things, Dodge City residents stepping out on their wives—Kate likely spent nights with all the above. She also spent some time honing her trade in Wichita. She likely met Earp in one place or the other, as he traversed them at the same time, but her denials of such led to speculation that the two may have had a romantic relationship. According to Kate, though, she was proudly independent and unattached.

In 1877 Kate turned up in Fort Griffin, Texas, and finally met a man who could keep up with her—Doc Holliday.

That autumn, when Kate met John Henry "Doc" Holliday dealing cards in Shanssey's Saloon, the connection was instant. Like Kate, Doc had an unforgettable face, with powerful cheekbones and a slick, black handlebar moustache. And, like Kate, Doc was well educated and from an affluent background. A native Georgian born to a well-to-do family, Doc had studied at the Pennsylvania College of Dental Surgery before returning to the South to work as a dentist in Atlanta. But—again like Kate—bad news had changed the course of his life. Diagnosed with tuberculosis in 1872, Doc's rattling cough forced him to close his dental practice. He then followed a physician's advice to move west to a drier climate for the sake of his lungs.

The heavy-drinking Doc found a new life in the saloons of the West. There was a steep learning curve: an educated Southern gentleman trading his books and dental tools for cards and guns. He once found himself in a gun battle with an equally sorry shot—the two fired back and forth without landing a single bullet—but Doc quickly developed into a sharpshooter. By the time he met Kate, the reckless Doc had killed men in Dallas, Denver, and elsewhere.

In Shanssey's Saloon, Doc worked the card table and Kate worked the male clientele, the two looking out for each other all the while—and forging a deep romantic bond.

By all accounts, the partnership between Kate and Doc was a tumultuous one—both drank too much, suffered bouts of

Portrait of Doc Holliday, the love of Big Nose Kate's life.
Kansas State Historical Society

depression, and were given to violent outbursts. They never officially married—neither the independent Kate nor the carpe diem Doc was suited for such an institution. But their on-again, off-again love affair would continue until death did them part.

Ed Bailey kept looking at the cards.

The pile of discards, which would provide Bailey valuable clues to help him win the poker game, was strictly off-limits. Doc, dealing to the man in Fort Griffin, called him out on his cheating. Bailey, a sour character, continued to look at the forbidden discards.

Doc warned him again.

Again, the gambler persisted.

Doc declared that the pot would be forfeited due to cheating. At this, Bailey pulled his gun. But Doc pulled his knife before the man could get off a shot, making a quick, deep gash across his stomach and disemboweling him.

The killing was in self-defense as far as Doc was concerned, and he went about his business. To his surprise, however, he was arrested and locked up in a Fort Griffin hotel (the town had no proper jail). This turn of events was particularly worrisome, as Doc wasn't a popular figure in town and would have little support at trial—if he didn't meet a lynch mob first.

Sensing her man's danger, Kate was determined to spring him from the hotel. She went to an old hay barn in town and, after setting the animals loose, lit the thing on fire. The barn quickly shot up in flames and seemed certain to catch the rest of the town on fire. The townspeople, including those who might have been tying a noose for Doc, were diverted to putting out the fire.

Meanwhile, Kate entered the hotel with two Colt revolvers, disarmed the man guarding Doc's room, and freed him. The pair hid in the darkness among the willow trees outside town. When the sun arose, Kate disguised herself in pants, boots, and a hat, and the pair set out on a pair of horses furnished by a friend of Kate's.

They journeyed to familiar stomping grounds—Dodge City, Kansas. Their first stop was Deacon Cox's boarding-house, where they registered as Dr. and Mrs. J. H. Holliday. Loving emotions were running high, as Doc was grateful for Kate's springing him from a potentially deadly situation. He declared that he would repay her by giving up gambling, the stressful occupation that involved too much whiskey and thus the threat of beatings for Kate. For her part, Kate swore off prostitution and the nightlife in general. Doc would open a dental practice once again, and Kate would be a respectable woman who kept house and took care of her man.

Kate and Doc moved into the Dodge House Hotel on the wild cow town's Front Street. Doc advertised his dentistry but before long was flipping cards at the Long Branch or Alhambra Saloon. Kate didn't keep her end of the bargain either; she went back to selling her body in the same places Doc ran poker and faro games. But things had changed since the couple had last provided their respective services in Dodge.

Earlier that year, 1878, Dodge City's city council had made both gambling and prostitution illegal. Of course both practices were rampant nonetheless, with card players and ladies of the night simply slapped with fines and then released to hit the saloons again. But Doc and Kate had extra protection from the ordinance. They had befriended one of Dodge's preeminent officers of the law, Wyatt Earp.

Doc and Earp got along famously. But their bond was truly sealed when Doc came upon a gang of Texas cowboys who had cornered Earp and meant to shoot him. Startling the cowboys, Doc bought Earp enough time to pistol-whip one assailant and send the rest packing. Earp felt indebted to Doc from that moment on, and the two would remain friends for many years.

Doc and Kate's connection was less stable. Their fights intensified, with Doc pummeling her or Kate threatening to kill him. Allie Earp, the second wife of Wyatt's brother Virgil, wrote that after one fight with her unofficial husband, Kate "looked as if an ore wagon had run over her. She had a black eye, one lip was swelled up, and her clothes looked like the wind had blown 'em on her ever which way."

At one point, Kate left Dodge, but before long she was back in Doc's room. Then it was Doc who left, this time for Las Vegas, where he was involved in a gunfight that left a man named Mike Gordan dead. Holliday fled yet another lynch mob and made it back to Dodge alive. But he found that his two closest friends, Earp and Kate, were gone.

Wyatt had left Dodge for Tombstone, Arizona, a new silver boomtown. Kate was headed in that general direction, stopping off in Prescott, Arizona, to earn some money in a brothel run by Bessie Earp. In January 1880 Doc left cold Kansas to find Kate in warm Arizona, and the two continued their fair-weather romance. Doc hit the lucky streak of his life-time, raking in as much as $40,000 at the card tables during a year or so in Prescott.

Both Doc and Kate finally joined Earp in Tombstone in 1880. Kate continued prostituting there and in surrounding towns. Meanwhile, the only thing worse than Doc's tuberculosis cough was Kate's drinking. In the early months of 1881, after Kate went on a particular nasty bender, Doc threw her out and declared their affair to be over forever. Kate was heartbroken.

Not long after the breakup, a stagecoach driver named Bud Philpot and his passenger were robbed and killed by masked men outside Tombstone. County Sheriff Behan and a group of locals who loathed Doc Holliday saw a chance to pin Doc with a crime. The sheriff hauled in Big Nose Kate, likely already drunk, and got her even drunker. Kate, burning with vengeful thoughts for her former lover, signed an affidavit declaring that Doc was one the masked murderers of the stage driver.

The *Tombstone Daily Nugget* reported on July 6, 1881, that a "warrant was sworn out yesterday before Judge Spicer for the arrest of Doc Holliday, a well-known character here, charging him with complicity in the murder of Bud Philpot and the attempted stage robbery near Contention some months ago, and he was arrested by Sheriff Behan. The warrant was issued upon the affidavit of Kate Elder, with whom Holliday had been living for some time past."

Judge Wells Spicer released Doc on a $5,000 bail posted by three friends, including Wyatt Earp. Earp's brother Virgil, the town marshal, put Kate behind bars to sober up and found a number of witnesses who could vouch that they were playing cards with Doc at the time of the stagecoach holdup. The Earps insisted that Kate's statement had been coerced and, for that matter, made while she was highly intoxicated. Indeed, once the liquor wore off, Kate retracted her accusation. The district attorney confirmed that no evidence incriminated Doc, and Judge Spicer dismissed the case.

But Kate was in her own legal trouble. She paid $12.50 to get out of jail for being "drunk and disorderly" and was charged with "threats against life," though the court commissioner threw the case out. The July 9 *Daily Nugget* relished the admonition of a lady of the night, calling Kate an "enraged and intoxicated woman."

After the headache was over, Wyatt Earp had a heart-to-heart with his friend Doc. "You send that fool woman away and I'll be satisfied," he said of Big Nose Kate.

Doc gave his volatile companion $1,000 and sent her out of town in a stagecoach. As one might imagine, Kate didn't stay gone.

According to her own writings later in life, she was back in Tombstone later that year when Doc helped the Earps in the famous gunfight at the O.K. Corral. She watched the bloodshed from Doc's apartment at Fly's Boarding House, she wrote, and welcomed a distraught Doc into her arms when the bullets were done flying.

The next year, 1882, Doc left Arizona to seek help for his tuberculosis in Sulfur Springs, Colorado. Kate's brother had a place in nearby Glenwood Springs, so she saw her mate frequently over the next several years as his condition worsened. Doc was arrested on Arizona murder warrants for his part in the O.K. Corral incident, but the Colorado governor wouldn't extradite the sick man. He died in a Colorado sanitarium in late 1887.

After Doc died, Kate's life calmed down considerably. She remained a somewhat impetuous character, but without equally volatile Doc to fan her fires, Kate's wildest days were behind her.

In 1888 Kate returned to Arizona, gave up prostitution, and earned a living cooking for area miners. She married a blacksmith, George Cummings, and the two lived in Bisbee, Arizona, a few miles from Tombstone, before moving to Pearce, yet another Arizona spot. But the marriage lasted only about a year. Cummings's drinking might have been acceptable; his spending Kate's own earnings on booze was not.

In 1889 Kate moved to the small town of Cochise, Arizona, where the Arizona Eastern and Southern Pacific Railroads met. In 1899 she was working as a clerk at John J. Rath's Cochise Hotel. At the turn of the twentieth century, the fifty-year-old Kate found work as a maid for John Howard in Dos Cabezas. She would live in his home for the next three decades, inheriting the property upon Howard's death. A year later Kate entered the Arizona Pioneers Home in Prescott, a state-run home for the elderly. There she would spend her final years documenting her privileged childhood, tragic adolescence, and wild youth with Doc Holiday.

Kate died in 1940, days before her ninetieth birthday. Her gravestone, which modestly memorializes a Mary K. Cummings, gives no hint that the woman buried there held many names—Mary Katherine Haroney, Katie Elder, Mrs. John Holliday, and of course Big Nose Kate.

The Masterson Brothers
Three to Draw To (1881 and 1893)

Families were usually large in the days of the westward movement, and they stuck together. As a general rule, blood *was* thicker than water, and close relatives looked out for one another, even if that meant breaking the law, even if you were a professional scumbag. Everybody's heard of the Earp boys, the James and Younger and Dalton brothers, the feuding Texas families. Later on, the quality diminished some—consider Ma Barker's feckless brood of killers—but in the heyday of the push west, there were some formidable family alliances involved.

As tough as they came were the Masterson boys—Jim, Ed, and of course Bat—immortalized after a fashion on the screen of your television set. Ed, the eldest, and Bat, the middle brother, were both born in Canada, Jim in rural Illinois. All the boys did part of their growing up in New York before the family moved to a farm near Wichita shortly after the close of the Civil War. They all hunted buffalo as very young men, then worked variously as small contractors, barkeeps, laborers, and, in Bat's case, army scout, before all of them turned to the hazardous trade of Kansas peace officer.

The Masterson brothers were a power to reckon with in early Kansas, men who laid their lives on the line repeatedly to enforce the law. They do not qualify as "outlaws" in the ordinary sense, but they were gunfighters of necessity, very tough hombres indeed. Because of this and because they made themselves part of enough private feuds, railroad wars, and a bitter, bloody county seat feud, they qualify for a place in this book. You simply can't talk about the violent history of frontier Kansas without talking about these three remarkable men.

All of them served the people of Dodge City, although not at the same time. Ed signed on in June of 1877, and after serving only some seven months, was elevated to the job of city marshal. He was only twenty-four, but very popular and highly respected by the people of Dodge. During the same period, brother Bat was elected Ford County sheriff, beginning in November of 1877.

That very month, Ed was called to the Lone Star Dance Hall to break up a pistol-waving quarrel between Bob Shaw and Texas Dick Moore, who seem to have been co-owners of the place. When Ed ordered Shaw to behave and give up his gun, Shaw instead took a shot at Texas Dick. Ed tried to cool the situation by bulldozing Shaw—clubbing him with his pistol barrel, a favorite tactic of frontier lawmen. The blow didn't seem to faze Shaw, who started firing on Ed, hitting him in the side and shoulder and paralyzing his gun arm. Ed coolly bent over, scooped up his revolver with his left hand, opened fire and hit Shaw twice, knocking him down. Moore and a casual bystander were also hit by somebody's bullets, but recovered. So did Shaw and Ed Masterson, who was soon back at work.

That was in November, and the following April Ed and Deputy Nat Haywood went to the Lady Gay saloon one evening to cool down a raucous gathering of six cowboys, one of whom, Jack Wagner, was also carrying a pistol in violation of a Dodge City ordinance. At first, all went well. Wagner was duly disarmed, and Ed gave Wagner's weapon to his boss, A. M. Walker. That should have ended the incident.

But it didn't. Instead of holding on to the weapon, protecting his man and everybody else, Walker not only gave the weapon back to Wagner, but joined him to charge the two lawmen. Ed wrestled with Wagner for the revolver, while Walker and other cowboys held off Deputy Haywood. Walker even tried to shoot Haywood in the face; the deputy was saved when the weapon misfired.

Meanwhile, Wagner managed to get off a shot that hit Ed Masterson in the gut, the muzzle-flash setting his clothing on fire. Ed drew his own gun and, in spite of his wound, hit Wagner once and Walker three times. Two bystanders were also wounded in the exchange. Wagner was finished, down and dying in nearby Peacock's Saloon, and Walker was suddenly fresh out of courage. He ran for his life, clear through Peacock's, and collapsed outside its back door. Walker survived, which, considering his actions in bringing on the fatal fight, was something of a shame.

Ed, his clothing still burning, walked some two hundred yards to another saloon and managed to say to the proprietor, "George, I'm shot," before he collapsed. He was carried to brother Bat's hotel room and was dead in half an hour. It is said that most of the town turned out for his funeral.

Bartholomew "Bat" Masterson—he later called himself William Barclay Masterson—was undoubtedly the most famous of the three brothers. Early in his career, while he was hunting buffalo, he was one of the party of hunters that beat off Quanah Parker's braves in the storied fight at Adobe Walls, out in the Texas panhandle. After a spell as an army scout, Bat drifted out

William Barclay "Bat" Masterson.
Kansas State Historical Society

of history for a couple of years, a period illuminated only by a gunfight between Bat and a soldier called King.

The cause was apparently King's jealousy over Bat keeping company with a lady named Molly Brennan. According to legend, King came raging into a saloon where Bat and Molly were billing and cooing, intending to use his trusty six-gun to unravel the triangle. He blazed away and in the resulting fight, both King and Molly died, Molly perhaps hit by a stray round from Bat's weapon. Bat was wounded, but that didn't hamper his aim. It did, according to legend, cause him to start using his trademark cane. The walking stick might have been the origin of his nickname "Bat," or maybe that was short for "battling," or simply some sort of contraction of "Bartholomew."

After his election as Ford County sheriff in late 1877, and Ed's murder, Bat stayed on in Dodge City and added to his credentials an appointment as a deputy U.S. marshal in January of 1879. Not long afterward, he abandoned his law enforcement responsibilities to go haring off with a number of other hired guns to the railroad right-of-way war in Colorado's Raton Pass. His employer, the Santa Fe Railroad, was successful in its contest with the Denver and Rio Grande, but Bat wasn't as lucky when he got back to Dodge and lost the next election. It is described as "hotly contested," and you have to think his absence from Dodge convinced some citizens that the sheriff's office needed new blood, or at least somebody who was around in case of need.

The next couple of years Bat wandered in New Mexico and Colorado, with a side trip up to Nebraska to help retrieve the wounded no-good Billy Thompson from a well-deserved lynching in Ogallala. Billy, wastrel brother of the deadly

Englishman Ben Thompson, was one of the West's notorious useless mouths, forever in trouble with somebody, only continuing to exist by the grace of people like Bat, doing a favor for Billy's far more likeable—and formidable—brother.

After some time in Kansas City, until early in 1881, Bat traveled to booming Tombstone to join some old Dodge friends, including Luke Short and Wyatt Earp. He wasn't long in Tombstone, for he was called back to Dodge City to back up brother Jim in a wild battle that erupted as soon as Bat got off the train. The fracas concerned a noxious bartender in Jim's Lady Gay Dance Hall and Saloon. Spying the bartender, Al Updegraff, and Jim's partner, A. J. Peacock, walking along the street, Bat famously yelled, "I have come over a thousand miles to settle this. I know you are heeled. Now fight!"—a greeting not calculated to soothe anybody's feelings. All three men opened fire, as did two more men in a saloon close by, one of whom was Jim Masterson. Somebody got a round into Updegraff and a bystander, who was running for his life at the time. Nobody was killed, and at an opportune moment the mayor and sheriff appeared with shotguns and enforced some order. Bat paid a small fine and got out of town forthwith.

The later years were kind to Bat Masterson. An accomplished writer and avid sportsman, he added newspaper sports writing to his achievements, along with sports-event promotions—largely boxing and racing—and acting as referee and judge. He married in 1891 and a decade later moved permanently to New York, of all places. There he spent his last twenty years contentedly writing sports columns for the *Morning Telegraph*. He died in harness, expiring quietly at his newspaper office desk in 1921.

Which leaves Jim Masterson, certainly the most active gunfighter of the clan. Like his brothers, he hunted buffalo for a while and then got into the entertainment business as co-owner—with A. J. Peacock—of the Lady Gay Dance Hall and Saloon in Dodge City. The Lady Gay seems to have thrived, in part because its entertainment featured singer Dora Hand, the toast of the frontier, stage-named Fannie Keenan. She deserves a word or two.

Dora was a real singer, classically trained in Europe, and truly became the toast of the town. Nearly everything written about her reflects genuine charm and beauty, phrases like "a beautiful creature," "classic beauty," and "queen of the fairy belles." There is some evidence that she even gave freely to charity. Mayor James "Dog" Kelley hired her away from the Lady Gay, paying the then-astronomical wage of $75 a week. Kelly was apparently romantically interested in Dora—which just maybe influenced the level of her pay—and his interest indirectly caused her untimely death at about thirty-four.

A cowhand named Kenedy was also panting after Dora, and after he and Kelly clashed and he was defeated, he carefully planned to murder his rival. Trouble was, he shot up Kelly's cabin when Kelly wasn't home but Dora was. She died instantly in her sleep. Kenedy seems to have escaped any punishment, some say due to a huge payoff to the court by his rich father.

Jim Masterson signed on as assistant marshal in June of 1878, working under tough Charlie Bassett, who had replaced Jim's murdered brother a scant two months before, and serving with none other than Wyatt Earp and his brother James. Wyatt and Jim were together during his first year of service, when a cowboy named Hoy and some friends starting shooting up the Comique Variety Hall. Jim and Wyatt were also in the line of fire and both returned fire, wounding Hoy, who lingered for a month, then died. Earp had long claimed and gotten the credit for the Hoy shooting, but it is just as likely that Masterson fired the fatal bullet.

The next couple of years were unremarkable, mostly arrests of drunken, roisterous cowhands—hundreds of them—plus at least one shooting in addition to Hoy, uneventful enough to be unremembered. The end of Jim's tenure came in the spring of 1881, when a change in city government heralded what its supporters would today call a "kinder, gentler era." It was not so for Jim Masterson, who got crossways with his business partner Peacock when Peacock hired his brother-in-law, one Al Updegraff, as bartender.

The falling-out was serious enough that it led to the inconclusive gunfight. Bat showed up in Dodge on the 16th of April, 1881 and had just gotten off the train when he saw Peacock and Updegraff. Jim and brother Bat forthwith became part of the monumental gunfight with Peacock and Updegraff and a couple of other men. When the smoke blew away, at least one bystander had been wounded, and Updegraff had taken a bullet through both lungs.

Jim next appears in the gunsmoke annals in 1889, as a hired gun in the Gray County War, one of the Midwest's perennial bitter contests to see which ambitious young town would rise to greatness and prosperity as the county seat. This contest was between the towns of Ingalls and Cimarron, only about six miles apart and bitter enemies. Now, the land records and such vital de facto indicia of government were zealously hoarded and protected in Cimarron. Therefore it seemed only logical to the men of Ingalls to go and get them.

And so they set out with a wagon, along with the Gray County clerk and some reliable shooters. These men were deputy sheriffs for the day, and included Jim Masterson and Bill Tilghman, among others. When they rolled into Cimarron and began to tote the records out of the Cimarron courthouse, the good men of Cimarron took umbrage, gathered into a defense force, and everybody began shooting. The invaders got away with just one seriously wounded man, plus minor injuries to Tilghman and the wagon driver. The defenders were battered: one man dead and three wounded, two seriously.

But as the lead flew through Cimarron and the Ingalls men retreated hastily, four of their partisans were left behind, barricaded in the courthouse; one was Jim Masterson. Surrounded, they at last surrendered the next day to the county sheriff. He turned out to be an Ingalls partisan and promptly turned them loose once they got out of Cimarron.

The same year, Jim became part of the great Oklahoma land rush, one of the very first settlers of the bustling town of Guthrie, which would become the first capital of Oklahoma Territory. There he served as deputy sheriff and was later appointed a deputy U.S. marshal in 1893. It was while he was serving as a U.S. officer that he was involved in the last major battle of his career.

It happened on the first of September, 1893, in the little town of Ingalls, down in Oklahoma Territory.

At the time, Ingalls could safely be called an outlaw town, periodic refuge to the notorious Doolin gang and divers hangers-on. There the gang could go to rest and carouse with some assurance of safety. They were a solid source of income to the people of Ingalls—real, hard U.S. money—and the outlaws were open-handed; after all, it's not hard to be generous with other people's money. And so the outlaws were not just tolerated in town, but welcomed by most of the tiny population.

The fact that Bill Doolin and his boys frequented Ingalls was not lost on the law, and the U.S. marshal for Oklahoma Territory determined to do something about it. And so a party of lawmen rode into little Ingalls on the first of September, 1893. One of that party was Deputy Marshal Jim Masterson.

The lawmen didn't have much luck, although most of them got into Ingalls unobserved. That changed when bandit George "Bitter Creek" Newcomb saw Deputy Marshal Tom Speed at the blacksmith shop, got suspicious, and went to investigate. When a boy pointed Bitter Creek out to the lawman and called him by name, Bitter Creek went for his rifle and Speed opened up; the very first round smashed into the outlaw's weapon and tore into his leg. But before Speed could fire again, things turned very bad indeed.

What the law had not anticipated was that outlaw Arkansas Tom Jones was still in his room in the woebegone frame building called the OK Hotel, and before Speed could finish the job on Bitter Creek, Arkansas Tom opened up from his window and hit the deputy marshal twice with rifle rounds. Speed went down in the dirt, dying, and the rest of the gang opened a fusillade from Ransome's Saloon to cover Bitter Creek's retreat.

The boy who had pointed out Bitter Creek to Speed was hit by a stray bullet, as was a salesman who unadvisedly ran out the saloon's back door. The boy would die; the salesman would survive a bullet in the liver. The bartender wisely forted up in the thick-walled icebox; the town drunk, one Newlin, was apparently so spifflicated that he slept through the whole war. When the smoke cleared, somebody counted 172 bullet holes in the saloon's plank walls.

The Doolin gang quickly concluded that it was time to go, and bolted from a shed attached to the saloon. A local, long on ingenuity and short on brains, provided them with a distraction when he stood in the saloon door with a rifle; that cost him three bullet wounds. But the outlaws made it, in spite of fire from the other lawmen. Arkansas Tom hit a second lawman, a bullet in the gut that would kill him the next day. The lawmen were still concentrating on the saloon, apparently unable to locate the source of Arkansas Tom's murderous fire.

Jim Masterson was trying to squeeze his body behind a tiny tree half as thick as he was while rifle fire tore chunks off his fragile shelter. Still another lawman went down, mortally wounded by Arkansas Tom's deadly Winchester, and then, about the time a courageous Masterson sprinted into the open, headed for the lawmen's wagon for more ammunition, the outlaws made their break. Galloping through a hail of fire, they got clear, although in the process outlaw Dynamite Dick was hit, sadly incurring only a nonfatal wound.

Arkansas Tom, the author of all this misery, was finished too. His friends had galloped off without him, and the furious lawmen were threatening to dynamite the whole OK Hotel. He gave it up, bound for a fifty-year sentence.

The town drunk at last awoke; he had missed the whole war, but was now horrified to find that "they shot my guts out!" . . . until he realized his fellow citizens had stuffed his pants full of chicken entrails while he dozed in the arms of Morpheus.

Ingalls was that kind of place. Sadly, nothing could bring back the dead lawmen, or the innocent boy, although retribution would find the rest of the gang members in time.

Ingalls was Jim Masterson's last big day as a peace officer, for those days were numbered. He remained a deputy marshal, and was still technically in harness the day he passed away in the spring of 1895 of "quick consumption." He would be missed. The Guthrie newspaper, the *Daily Oklahoma State Capital*, characterized him pretty well: "When every man would flinch, he would still be found in the front rank . . . Jim Masterson was a man who never went back on a friend, and never forgot an obligation."

A pretty fair epitaph.

Luke Short
The Deadly Ladies' Man, 1883

Luke Short was courteous, well-dressed, soft-spoken, and charming. He was also as tough as they came, one of that rare breed who never seemed to lose composure in the face of danger. He never picked a fight but once, but he finished quite a number of them, and lost none; he never went looking for trouble, but never ran away from it either. The ladies liked him a lot, for he was very much a gentleman, polite and well-spoken, who treated the fair sex as they wanted to be treated, qualities not always found out on the raw edges of America.

He did not dash about on the frontier bashing people with his cane, like Bat Masterson on television, but for the frontier, he was Beau Brummell. He wasn't physically imposing, just five feet six inches and about 125 pounds, but even so, as men said in those days, he was "all wool and a yard wide." Sartorially speaking, he was a sight to gladden the eye—top hat, cane, and all. His well-cut suits were only slightly modified, having an extra-long right-front pants pocket, leather-lined to caress his revolver and make his draw smoother and an instant quicker.

Luke Short was born back in 1854, a Mississippi kid transplanted to Texas when he was very small. In his teenage years he pushed cattle north to the railroad towns, then went to whiskey peddling up in Nebraska. The customers were Indians—selling booze to them was a violation of federal law—and Short

Luke Short.
Western History Collections, University of Oklahoma Libraries, Ferguson 294

later said he'd had to kill some half-dozen drunk customers in the line of business. Avoiding federal arrest, Short spent some time scouting and dispatch riding for the army, gambled in booming Leadville, then spent a couple of years in Dodge City, working as a dealer in the Long Branch Saloon.

Up until that time, Short had been in only one recorded shooting affair, a "minor" matter in which he wounded and discouraged his opponent. All that changed in 1881, when Short went to Tombstone. He dealt in the Oriental Saloon, along with Doc Holliday, Bat Masterson, and Wyatt Earp—fast company, that—and killed his first man in 1881 when he got edgewise with a gambler named Charlie Storms.

The falling-out had something to do with a card game. The first confrontation between the two men was broken up by Bat Masterson, but when Storms later unwisely returned to the Oriental and recommenced the falling-out, both men went for their guns. Now the world saw another side to pleasant, courteous Luke Short. He "charged" Storms, breaking his opponent's neck with one round and driving a second through the gambler's heart, whereof he expired. Legend has it that Luke then turned to Masterson and said, "You sure pick some of the damnedest friends, Bat."

Short was back in Dodge City by 1883, when he bought Chalk Beeson's interest in the fabled Long Branch, but trouble followed him. The city authorities had arrested three women employed by the Long Branch, officially called "singers" but more remuneratively employed in a rather more horizontal posture. Luke took umbrage at the arrest, a distinct obstacle to commerce, especially since several of his competitors employed "singers" and none of them were arrested, including what the paper called "a whole herd" employed by one competing saloon.

That led inevitably to a clash with the "reform element" and a gunfight of sorts with L. C. Hartman, who held the curious dual office of city clerk and special policeman. Passing before a darkened store with another man, Short spied Hartman. Saying to a companion, "There's one of the sons-of-bitches; let's throw it to him," he fired at Hartman, who dove for cover, unhurt. As Short turned to leave, Hartman pulled down on him, also without result.

No hits, no runs, no errors, but Short was forced to leave town by the city fathers. He did, but he was just getting started. Lawyers for both sides argued, Luke petitioned the state governor for relief, and that worthy readied the National Guard to intervene in Dodge and demanded to know why town officials thought they could simply exile people without trial.

The rulers of Dodge at first would not budge, so Short called on his friends and returned to Dodge with a whole phalanx of the faithful. The formidable reinforcement included, among others, Bat Masterson, Wyatt Earp, Bill Tilghman, Charlie Bassett, Shotgun Collins, and Rowdy Joe Lowe, none of them rank amateurs at the gun-fighting profession.

A good many lesser-known fighting men also showed up, according to the newspapers, including such ominous names as Six-Toed Pete, Dynamite Sam, Dirty Sock Jack, Blackjack Bill, and Dark Alley Jim. This formidable array—at least those gathered by Short—collectively called itself the "Dodge City Peace Commission," and peace indeed there was after the city government realized how badly it was outgunned. Petitions and telegrams flew in both directions amid predictions of rivers

Dodge City Peace Commission (1883) members are identified as (back row, left to right) William H. Harris, Luke Short, and William "Bat" Masterson; (front row, left to right) Charles E. Bassett, Wyatt Earp, Frank McLain, and Neil Brown.
Western History Collections, University of Oklahoma Libraries, Campbell 616

of blood, but apparently nobody in Dodge was anxious to try conclusions with this young army.

The newspapers had a field day, speculating about the number of men the invaders had killed wherever they had been before. Bat Masterson was a favorite, and speculation as to the number of dead men for whom he was responsible ranged from "a man for every year of his life" to "at least a dozen," or maybe the death toll was twenty-six, or . . .

In the end, the quarrel with the city magnates ended, as T. S. Eliot wrote, "not with a bang but a whimper." There was some sort of out-of-court settlement; Luke Short shook the dust of Dodge City from his polished shoes and went off to try his luck in Fort Worth. There he acquired a piece of the booming White Elephant Saloon, a mistress called Hettie, and a substantial chunk of money. He also acquired another scalp, that of professional bad man and general pain-in-the-neck "Long-Haired Jim" Courtright.

Courtright called himself a detective; in fact, he ran a profitable protection racket, and one of his customers was the White Elephant. Now, Luke wanted no part of paying, and even though he finally sold his interest in the White Elephant, he got threats from Courtright, and at length the two met at, of all places, a shooting gallery. A few more words were exchanged, and it all came unstuck when Luke reached inside his coat. Courtright yelled at him not to pull his pistol; Luke answered that he "never carried a gun there," but Long-Haired Jim was already digging for a revolver.

What happened next was an object lesson for the maxim that haste makes waste, for one story of the fight tells that Courtright's pistol hammer caught in the chain of his own watch. Luke got his own weapon clear and emptied it, the first round smashing the cylinder of Courtright's pistol and tearing off one of his thumbs. Two rounds missed but three more hit Courtright as he reached for a second revolver, one of them in the heart. The encounter was widely reported, like this tongue-in-cheek passage from the *Syracuse Times*, which noted that the killing reduced the number of "professional killers of the West to a quartet." It continued:

> There used to be more, but the same wise Providence
> that disintegrated the Jesse James gang and distributed it
> among the cemeteries, penitentiaries and dime museums
> of the land had elected that bad men eventually kill
> each other. Thus the supply has been kept ahead of the
> demand.

One more gunfight remained in Short's career, caused (of course) by another quarrel over gambling. This time his opponent was Charlie Wright, a saloon owner, and he opened up on Short from behind with a shotgun. Now, anybody who can't kill his quarry *with a shotgun from behind* ought to stay out of the assassination business altogether, and that included Wright, who managed to inflict only an inconsequential leg wound. Wright fled, and was lucky to escape with no more than a wrist broken by one of Luke's pistol bullets.

Just three years later, Luke Short was dead of what was then called "dropsy," more accurately congestive heart disease. With his brother and his wife beside him, he died quietly at little Geuda Springs, Kansas, then known as a spa, a place of peace and healing waters. He was only thirty-nine.

The *Dodge City Democrat* mourned his exodus in glowing terms: "Thus ends the life of one of the most noted and daring men in the west." Especially considering the tall dogs Luke ran with, it was the highest possible praise.

Henry Brown
Good Rifle, Bad Marshal, 1884

On the first day of 1883, the town of Caldwell presented its beloved new marshal with a fine gift—a customized rifle. It was a fitting gift for a man whose line of work called for top-notch weaponry. And it was a beauty. The Winchester featured inlays of precious metals—silver and gold—and a lovely silver plate engraved with a sincere tribute: "Presented to city marshal H. N. Brown for valuable services rendered in behalf of the citizens of Caldwell Kas." The inscription included the name of the town's approving mayor, A. M. Colson. Marshal Henry Brown was the toast of Caldwell.

Caldwell was a particularly raunchy cow town just north of Indian Territory. Reckless cowboys, six-shooters never far from their dirty hands, menaced morally upright citizens and had their run of the saloons. Then Henry Brown rode into town. He had served as deputy sheriff of Oldham County in Texas, and he had a cool, quiet, commanding presence. In June 1882 Caldwell hired Brown as assistant marshal. He quickly made a name for himself as a tough customer, a fast draw, and a reasonable official. Six months later he received his big promotion and his gorgeous rifle.

Brown brought Ben Wheeler—an impossibly tall stretch of a Texas man—to town to serve as his deputy, and together they tamed one of the wildest towns in the West. Gun ordinances were enforced. Unruly drunks were jailed. Violent offenders were arrested. Weary Caldwell residents saw true order and civility for the first time, and Brown's popularity only grew. When he killed two renegades in the line of duty, the town applauded. Just a year after his appointment as marshal, Brown married and bought a house, delighting the town with his obvious intentions to stay in Caldwell. After living in fear of bandits, drunks, and wayward cowboys, residents felt lucky to have a hero in their midst.

Had they only known.

Henry Brown might have cleaned up Caldwell, but his own past was very, very dirty.

Brown was born in 1857 in Cold Spring Township, Missouri, and was orphaned as a child. He stayed with his sister on their uncle's farm close to Rolla, Missouri, until he was seventeen, at which point Brown rode west to see where life might take him. It was 1875, and the frontier promised adventure.

Brown found work on a ranch in eastern Colorado and then hunted buffalo for some time. In 1876, though, he found himself in trouble in the Texas panhandle. He killed a man there and headed farther west to Lincoln County, New Mexico.

In New Mexico Brown got on with a rancher named L. G. Murphy. He worked for Murphy for a year and a half, during which time Murphy was embroiled in a bitter battle with competing ranchers John Chisum and John Tunstall and lawyer Alexander McSween. When Tunstall was murdered, a gang of his supporters formed—including a young fellow known as Billy the Kid. In early 1878 Brown, angry over a salary dispute, dumped Murphy and joined Billy's group, known as the Regulators. Violence over cattle ranges, known today as the Lincoln

County War, then raged for weeks. Brown was indicted with two others for the murders of Sheriff William Brady and Deputy George Hindman. He managed to evade law officers, though, and hit the trail with Billy the Kid.

By the fall of that year, Brown had plenty of blood on his hands, and he fit right in with Billy the Kid and fellow gang members John Middleton, Tom O'Folliard, and Fred Wait. The Lincoln County War and the New Mexico law behind them, the group stole an entire herd of horses and made their way to the area of Tascosa, Texas. At this point, Billy and O'Folliard daringly returned to New Mexico, Middleton to his home in Kansas and Wait to his home in Oklahoma. The gang had dissolved; so too had Brown's patience for the outlaw life.

Staying on in Tascosa, Brown worked as a cowhand for George Littlefield before taking supremely ironic work tracking horse thieves. His next job, as deputy sheriff of Oldham County, was short-lived, and he drifted north to work for ranch foreman Barney O'Connor in Indian Territory. Finally, a bit farther north, he was in Caldwell, offering a very selective résumé to the townspeople and receiving the marshal's star-shaped badge.

Henry Brown seemed to be the answer to Caldwell's prayers. His square jaw and stern face belied his criminal past. It's been said that one resident, small business owner Charles Siringo, might have known Brown's true identity. Siringo had helped track Billy the Kid some years ago and might have crossed paths with Brown. If that's the case, he didn't share the information, perhaps fearing for his own life. Besides, it was information the town of Caldwell didn't want to hear. Brown was their knight in a shining badge. He had helped a federal deputy marshal capture a band of horse thieves in nearby Hunnewell.

He had killed what the town thought to be a menacing Pawnee Indian brandishing a gun in the town grocery. He had used his rifle to shoot down a drunken Texas gambler making threats against the town. Yes, Brown was a good marshal.

So when Brown requested permission from the mayor to leave Caldwell and track down a wanted man in Indian Territory, the mayor agreed. He knew Brown had fallen into debt, and the $1,200 bounty on the man's head would come in handy. Could he take his deputy, Ben Wheeler? Sure. Wheeler's real name was William Robinson, and Brown had met him during his outlaw days in Texas. Again, Caldwell was none the wiser.

In late April 1884, Brown, Wheeler, and two mustached cowboys, William Smith and John Wesley, rode out of Caldwell with extra horses in tow, they were headed for Medicine Lodge, Kansas, seventy miles west of Caldwell.

As they neared the town they entered the Gypsum Hills— slopes, small canyons, and buttes of red dirt just north of what is now Oklahoma. It was a curious landscape with sinkholes and natural bridges, and its many caves were ideal for waiting out the night with the snakes and prairie dogs. The men tied their extra horses in a shallow canyon and readied themselves for a big day.

In a torrential downpour on the morning of April 30, the men made a mental note of their hidden horses' location and rode toward Medicine Lodge. It was miserable weather, turning the earth into a red paste, but fine conditions for their plans that day—sheets of rain meant that the riders might go completely unnoticed about town.

Brown and his men hitched their horses behind a shed near Medicine Lodge Bank. Around 9:00 a.m. they burst into the bank with guns drawn—Brown's fine Winchester gleaming—and demanded money. Bank president E. W. Payne reached for his gun, but Brown shot first and killed him. Cashier George Geppert threw his hands up, but another member of the outlaw gang shot him anyway. Before he collapsed and died, Geppert lunged for the vault and locked it, ensuring that the robbers wouldn't get what they had come for. For Brown, that was money to pay off his debts.

Outside the bank, the thieves had more trouble awaiting them. Due to the rainstorm, a pack of cowboys was waiting out the bad weather in a livery stable across the road from the bank. They had meant to join a roundup at nearby Antelope Flat, but for now they sought refuge from the storm. Thus they heard the gunshots at the bank and saw Brown's group making off on their horses. Several of the cowboys mounted up and followed the outlaws at breakneck pace out of Medicine Lodge. The rain hadn't worked to Brown's advantage at all.

The pursuit lasted for two hours, pushing the men's horses to exhaustion. Brown and the three others made their way across the sometimes-confusing formations of red earth to the canyon where they had hidden fresh horses. Unbeknownst to them, the landowner had moved a fence they had used to mark their horses' spot. They rode into the wrong box canyon, which was more than thirty feet deep. By the time they realized their mistake, they were trapped within the canyon's high walls, their horses growing anxious as water from the downpour collected at their hooves. A posse of nine men—led by Barney O'Connor, who had once hired Brown as a cowboy—had them cornered. As the canyon flooded, Brown and then Wheeler, Smith, and Wesley gave themselves up.

The proud posse that captured Henry Brown and company in the Gypsum Hills near Medicine Lodge (rear, left to right: Tom Doran, Barney O'Connor, Alex McKinney, Vernon Lytle; middle, left to right: Lee Bradley, Roland Clark, Wayne McKinney; seated, left to right: George Friedly and John Fleming). *Kansas State Historical Society*

The posse and their captives returned to Medicine Lodge. When they arrived in town, it was still light outside, and the prisoners posed in their leg irons for a very glum photograph in which Brown still wears the handkerchief he had surely pulled over his face during the robbery. The crowd shouted for the men to be hanged, but the robbers were locked up in the Medicine Lodge jail.

Inside the log structure, the men had a much-needed meal and Brown wrote a letter to his new wife, Maude. "This is hard for me to write this letter but, it was all for you, my sweet wife, and for the love I have for you," he wrote. "If a mob does not kill us we will come out all right after while. Maude, I did not shoot any one, and did not want the others to kill any one but they did, and that is all there is about it." Brown went on to instruct her to sell his possessions to cover any existing debts. But not the Winchester rifle, he instructed. That item was too special to pawn.

Wheeler made attempts at a letter to his own wife, but he was a blubbering mess and couldn't write anything coherent. The tension he'd felt in the crowd of locals seemed to promise death. J. J. Burns, editor of the nearby *Belle Plaine News*, also sensed something foreboding when reporting the incident. "Citizens immediately organized and followed the outlaws," Burns wrote, "and before this they are probably hanging from a tree."

Darkness fell on the town, and by 9:00 p.m. the prisoners' fears were realized. An angry mob of citizens was at the jail door, hungry for vigilante justice. Firing their weapons, they overpowered the guards and busted inside.

In the chaos Brown made a break for it, but a local farmer with a sawed-off double-barrel shotgun had other ideas. He pumped Brown full of bullets—the crooked marshal collapsed, dead at the age of twenty-six.

Wheeler took the chance to make his own escape, fleeing in the opposite direction, but a gun flash set his vest on fire and made a bright, obvious target against the night sky. He ended up with three bullets in his torso, a shattered right arm, and bloody stumps where two fingers once resided on his left hand.

Bleeding and in agony, Wheeler was dragged with Smith and Wesley to a tall elm tree. Long ropes were thrown over a sturdy branch. Wheeler begged for his life, promising to disclose information "that would interest the community at large" if he were spared. But the mob would have none of it. They strung him up with the other two. The three bodies were left hanging from the tree, a warning to any other would-be robbers.

Today the spot where Brown and his comrades found themselves trapped is known as Jackass Canyon. As for Brown's Winchester, his widow did get rid of it. The rifle made its way through several hands before ending up at the Kansas Museum of History in Topeka.

Dave Mather
Mysterious Dave (1885)

He doesn't have the "rep" that a lot of others have, like the Earps or the Mastersons or "Bear River" Tom Smith; nobody is sure how he got his nickname of Mysterious Dave, either: there really wasn't much mysterious about him except maybe that he didn't talk much, and nothing at all that anybody could call romantic. He was as deadly as any of them, though, and a whole lot less likeable. His family name was Mather, of the famous family that had produced the brothers Increase and Cotton. He was proud of his heritage, although his sea captain father was nothing to brag about, having abandoned his family and gotten himself stabbed to death in Shanghai by a ship's cook.

Dave Mather's heritage was well known, especially once he got a reputation for excellence at shooting people. Said the Dodge City *Kansas Cowboy*,

> Old Cotton is dead, or ought to be by this time . . . wrote a book on witchcraft, in which he proved conclusively there were numerous and divers witches around Salem who were doing more deviltry than his descendant, Dave, ever did in Dodge City . . . when a man got possessed in Dodge, Dave pulled his little gun and put an end to him.

After going to sea briefly with his brother—until they jumped ship—Dave turned bad if he wasn't already. Some history has him rustling cattle in Arkansas along with "Dirty

Dave" Rudabaugh, a monumentally nasty piece of work, and somebody called Milt Yarberry. He may have committed his first murder then, or at least been an accessory, for a warrant was issued for all three men for the robbery and killing of a rancher. The three chose not to wait around and try conclusions before a jury.

Mather hunted buffalo for a time on the Llano Estacado and was in Dodge City early in the 1870s, in time to run on down into Texas to sell phony gold bricks with Wyatt Earp around Mobeetie. At the end of the decade he was in the Colorado country as a hired gun during the "railroad wars," a vicious competition for rights-of-way. Other stars among the railroad soldiers were Rudabaugh, Doc Holliday, and the deadly Englishman, Ben Thompson.

By 1879 he had become a sort of lawman by joining the "Dodge City Gang," which in spite of its nickname ran the rackets in Las Vegas, New Mexico. The evil genius down in Las Vegas was the justice of the peace, of all things, an ugly character christened Hyman Neill, better known by his *nom de crime* "Hoodoo Brown." Mather got himself appointed deputy U.S. marshal and got to run again with the egregious Dirty Dave Rudabaugh, who got his name not only from his poisonous personality but also from his penetrating odor, which preceded him, some said, by a quarter of an hour.

While acting as a deputy marshal, or maybe it was as local constable, Mysterious Dave rid the earth of a railroad gang boss named Costello (or Castello). Costello was trying to separate two of his quarrelsome men—drunk, of course—and both he and they were waving pistols about when Dave showed up and commanded everybody to cease and desist and put away their

Dave Mather.
Kansas State Historical Society

weapons. Costello took umbrage at this, pointed his revolver at Dave, and said, "Not a step closer," or something equally foolish. *Exit* Costello.

Later that same year, 1880, Mysterious Dave tried a different line of work, leaving in a wagon "well equipped" to go prospecting in the Gunnison area of Colorado. That did not last long, for before year's end he was back in Las Vegas. While he was there, he was involved in a memorable fight in a dive called the Close and Patterson Variety Hall. The town marshal, Joe Carson, was killed in a battle with four obstreperous cowboys who had already spent a goodly portion of the day emptying bottles. Mather—maybe Carson's deputy, maybe not—took on all four, and when the smoke blew away, one was down and dying, a second was on the ground badly wounded, and the other two had taken flight.

Later captured, the last two cowboys and the wounded man were unceremoniously jerked from their cells for a communal lynching at the plaza windmill; they died all right, but not by the rope. Before the town could formally stretch their necks, Mrs. Carson appeared and she and her trusty gun got that satisfaction.

A variation on that tale has it that Mysterious Dave showed up as Carson lay dying and vowed to the lawman that he would avenge him. Whereat Mather went off to the saloon and blew away the whole crowd . . . only in this version the killers were called the "Henry gang" and numbered seven. Dave got 'em all, in this story, although how he did it is not specified: Did he have two revolvers, or reload on the run; did he get two with a single bullet, or did he simply scare one of them to death . . . ?

In 1880 Las Vegas finally had enough of the Dodge City Gang. Hoodoo Brown and Dirty Dave went to jail (both later escaped), and Mather moved on to booming San Antonio, Dallas, and Fort Worth. There he is said to have had a flaming romance with Georgia Morgan, madam of a busy Dallas bordello called the Long Branch. When the affair finally cooled, Dave moved on, but he took with him not only Georgia's affection, but divers items of her jewelry.

That ungentlemanly act moved her to follow him, a woman not only both scorned and robbed, but also armed with both butcher knife and gun; she was, as a newspaper commented, "looking for her Davey." Fortunately for Dave, the law reached her before she found him. As the *Fort Worth Democrat-Advance* neatly put it, "Not being used to seeing a female armory walking on the streets, Georgia was captured and placed in the calaboose, to be kept as a curiosity."

And so Dave survived to take his talent to Kansas, specifically Dodge City, where he became the owner of the Opera House Saloon. There also he took sides in the altercation between the mayor, Larry Deger, and Luke Short, who by then owned the famous Long Branch. In particular, Dave got crossways with Tom Nixon, owner of a saloon called the Lady Gay, a direct competitor to Dave, who owned the Opera House Saloon. The two clashed outside the Opera House. Nixon shot once at Mather, but Dave's only injuries were a powder-burned face and a little finger damaged by a splinter. The *Dodge City Democrat* wisely opined that the end of the clash was "by all appearances not yet," and sure enough, it wasn't. Only three days later, Mather killed Nixon deader than a nit, shooting him four times, the last three as he lay on the floor.

The town consensus seems to have been that the earlier shot fired by Nixon meant Nixon would continue to be dangerous to Mather; ergo, in the quaint reasoning of the frontier, Mather's shooting of Nixon was really in self-defense. Therefore, there would be no official retribution. The next year, 1885, Mather was again charged with murder after a gambler named Dave Barnes ended up a corpse on the floor of the Junction Saloon.

The two had been playing cards and an argument ensued. The facts of what followed were impossible to sort out, outside of the plain fact that Barnes was rendered dead. Dave suffered a bullet-graze to the head and was arrested, but held only until it developed that he had not even gotten off a shot. Probably he hadn't because his brother Josiah had permanently perforated the victim.

The *Kinsley Mercury* likened Dave's hurried departure to a more famous flight: "Dave Mather left Dodge City last Wednesday night as Jeff Davis left the Southern Confederacy . . . it had come time to kill Dave, and not desiring to be present on that occasion, he disguised himself as Jeff Davis and walked. His whereabouts will probably be known when it comes time for his next killing."

Dave Mather's time in Dodge produced a charming story of his encounter with an itinerant preacher, who understandably resented Dave showing up spiffflicated at a revival. When he remonstrated with Dave over his condition, Dave rose to his feet and declared he was saved and was ready to die, along with anybody else who wanted to. When he began to shoot out the lights, a great exodus of the faithful followed, including the preacher. Scoffing, Dave departed.

When it was time to hit the road again, Mysterious Dave vanished, apparently undisguised. This time it would be for "parts unknown," for there is a report that he skipped town owing some $3,000 in bail money. Just where he went and how he ended his mortal run is not clear to this day: He probably held down a job as deputy marshal in New Kiowa, Kansas, for a year or so, beginning in the summer of 1885. Then . . . nothing.

It has been said that he died in 1886; if this tale is true, he died as he lived, by the gun, and his body was left lying on the railroad tracks. Another tale has him joining the Royal Canadian Mounted Police and serving as a Mountie into the early 1920s. Maybe so, but this one seems pretty far-fetched, since the Mounted Police had very high standards, as they do today. They would be unlikely to accept anybody with a record remotely representing Mather's, at least if they took the trouble to find out who he was, where he'd been, and what he'd done.

His brother, dying in 1932, was asked what became of Dave. "We do not know what happened to Dave," he said. "We wish we knew."

To much of the rest of the West, it was good riddance.

Emmett Dalton
From Holdups to Hollywood, 1892

Bob Dalton wanted to outdo Jesse James.

As the leader of the infamous Dalton Gang, which had terrorized the West and evaded the law for two years, Bob had grown cocky. The wildest of the bunch, he had plans to make a legend of the Dalton name. In October 1892 he told his brothers-in-crime that they would rob not one bank but *two banks at once.*

In broad daylight.

In their own hometown of Coffeyville, Kansas.

"I tried to persuade him not to try it," his youngest brother, Emmett, would tell a reporter as he lay bleeding in a Coffeyville jail, "but did not succeed, as he had a grudge against the town and wanted revenge for what he had heard the people here were saying and trying to do about us."

The Dalton family had come to Coffeyville, a booming town of 2,300 people in southeast Kansas, in 1886. It was a large brood. James and Adeline Dalton had fifteen children, four of whom would gain outlaw infamy: Gratton, Bob, Emmett, and Bill. (Their bandit ways were in their blood. Their mother, Adeline, was aunt to the famous Younger boys—Cole, Bob, and Jim—who rode with Frank and Jesse James.)

The Dalton brothers were teenagers and young men when their family ended up in Coffeyville, and the area was a wild place to come of age. Just a few miles north of Oklahoma—then

Indian Territory—Coffeyville was part of the frontier, and the bloody Civil War years were a very recent memory. It was a violent time, and citizens were either on the right or wrong side of the law.

In the Daltons' case, they tried both sides.

Older brother Frank served as a federal deputy marshal in Fort Smith, Arkansas, taking teenage brother Bob along on many of his dangerous missions. The job was short-lived—Frank was shot and killed in a gunfight with the Smith-Dixon Gang in November 1887.

Grat filled his dead brother's shoes as a deputy marshal in Fort Smith and then in 1889 for the Muskogee court in Indian Territory. That same year, Bob was commissioned as a deputy marshal for the federal court in Wichita. But the lawman acts didn't hold up for long.

Stationed in the Osage Nation, Bob killed his first man at the age of nineteen—an incident he claimed was in the line of duty—but rumors flew that he had abused his power and killed an innocent man over a girl.

In spring 1890 Bob was charged with selling liquor in Indian Territory. Instead of appearing in court, he went on the lam. Later that year, Grat was arrested for horse theft but managed to escape lynching.

Bob and Grat had lost any respect in the town of Coffeyville. Plus, their father had recently died. They were mad at the world, and their days as lawmen were over.

Bob and Grat banded together with Emmett, the youngest Dalton child, who had been working as a cowboy. Emmett looked the part of the little brother—he had chubby cheeks, even in adulthood, which gave him a youthful appearance despite his tall stature and receding hairline. Together they recruited other gunmen from the ranches Emmett had worked: George "Bitter Creek" Newcomb, Bill McElhanie, "Blackfaced Charley" Bryant, Bill Doolin, Charlie Pierce, Dick "Texas Jack" Broadwell, and Bill Powers.

This rotating cast of characters robbed trains of thousands of dollars from Arkansas to California—a Santa Fe train at Wharton, another passing through Indian Territory, a train station near the Arkansas border. At one point Grat was arrested for a Southern Pacific train holdup in California, but he escaped officials by jumping out of the train into the San Joaquin River. The Dalton Gang seemed invincible.

On the morning of October 5, 1892, five members of the gang rode into the Daltons' old stomping ground of Coffeyville: Grat, Bob, and Emmett Dalton along with "Texas Jack" and Bill Powers.

Emmett claimed he was a reluctant participant. "I had no money to leave the country on, and I also did not think we could get away if we came," he would say later that day.

But his close brother Bob, just a year older, believed Emmett was essential to the robbery's success.

"We knew the lay of the land thoroughly, and it was agreed that Bob and I should take the First National and the other three boys Condon's Bank," said Emmett, twenty-one years old. "Bob thought he and I were better than any six of the others, and knowing the First National to be the hardest to rob, we selected that and assigned Condon's to the others."

The five men tied their horses in an alley and entered the two banks. Bob and Emmett got to work filling bags at First

National, while the rest waited for the Condon Bank cashier to open the safe—the cashier lied that the lock had a time delay, and the robbers sat waiting. Meanwhile, unbeknownst to them, a group of armed men was making its way to the town square. The Daltons had been recognized as they rode through town, and officials had been notified.

Bob and Emmett, indeed the more skilled of the group, left First National with more than $20,000. For good measure, they took the bank employees with them to the entrance. Seeing armed men in the square, however, they made a break for their horses. Bob did not make it far—he was shot in the head by a townsman and died instantly.

Emmett reached his horse but, seeing his fallen brother, hesitated long enough to be shot in the right arm and right hip and take twelve rounds of buckshot to the back.

The other robbers heard the gunfire from Condon Bank and fired from the windows. Their bullets struck the cashier of the First National Bank, still standing on the bank's steps, as well as a local shoemaker who had joined the group of avengers. The three men fled the bank, firing as they ran for their horses. Texas Jack and Bill Powers were the first among them to fall. Grat Dalton made it to the alley, where he shot and killed the city marshal but ultimately died himself.

The final death toll: four bandits and four residents of Coffeyville. Three more, including the cashier were wounded. All the stolen money—$20,240 from First National Bank and about $3,000 from Condon Bank—was returned, along with several hundred dollars the gang had on them at the time.

The next morning, officials lined up the four dead criminals outside the city jail, and hundreds of people came to gawk and

Dead members of the Dalton Gang following their failed bank robbery in Coffeyville; clockwise from bottom left: Bob Dalton, Bill Powers (aka Tim Evans), Dick Broadwell (aka Texas Jack), Grat Dalton. *Kansas State Historical Society*

to try to get a peek at Emmett Dalton, who had survived two Winchester bullets and a spray from a shotgun. Emmett cried when his dead brothers were hauled into his cell for identification. But no one mourned their burial later that day in the Dalton plot of the city cemetery.

The fallen citizens of Coffeyville were of great concern of course. Railroad companies that had offered rewards for killing the Dalton brothers were asked to award those amounts to the families of the dead. (Decades later, the town would open the Dalton Defenders Museum in their honor.) Meanwhile, talk of seizing and lynching Emmett circled the town, but officials guarded his cell as he lay quietly.

Emmett wasn't lynched for his involvement in the bank robberies. In fact, word spread that he was a model captive,
agreeable, even gregarious. Many pointed out that Emmett
himself hadn't killed anyone in the gun battle. Townspeople
remembered him as the most kindhearted of the Dalton
bunch. Before long, anger had turned to near sympathy. This
description by a reporter from nearby Independence summed
up the popular sentiment:

> Through the kindness of Sheriff Callahan we were
> permitted to visit the office of Dr. Wells, when Emmett
> Dalton was under examination. We saw a young man
> lying on a bed who had just reached his majority. He
> had rather an attractive face, a mild, clear eye, good
> complexion, regular features, and a voice as smooth and
> pleasant as a man often possesses. There was nothing
> coarse, nor brutal, nor villainous looking about him. A
> man would indeed have been hard hearted, who could
> have witnessed the ordeal through which he went without
> feeling a pity in his heart.

Nine days after the shootout, Emmett was moved to the
Independence jail, where he quickly gained favor and might
even have sparked the passions of lonely women imagining
a handsome, gentle desperado in need of love. One visiting
newspaper writer for the *Vinita Indian Chieftain* cautioned
against such romantic notions.

> . . . Emmett is still improving and will undoubtedly
> recover. His cell is brightened by bouquets of beautiful
> flowers sent him by foolish women and he is having what
> many people think an easy time of it when it is considered
> that three widows and one poor old mother mourn their
> husbands and son by reason of the Dalton raid.

A writer for the *Independence Star and Kansan* the next day denied the existence of any such bouquets or plush treatment.

Meanwhile, Emmett's mother and eldest brother, who had cared for her and their farm since the father's death, came and went. Emmett's older brother Bill, who had served as a lawman in California, traveled to ensure Emmett's proper defense and even brought suit against the town for robbing his dead brothers' bodies of $900. Emmett himself spent the rest of the year recovering from his wounds.

In January Emmett reluctantly pled guilty to second-degree murder, despite claiming that he had never fired his gun during the Coffeyville incident. The judge sentenced him to life in prison, and he cried as he was hauled to the state penitentiary in Leavenworth.

Emmett spent the next fourteen years there in a small cell, demonstrating good behavior and writing letters asking for his release.

In 1907 Emmett was granted parole in order to travel to Topeka for surgery on his right arm, which had never completely healed from its rifle wound. He continued to impress everyone he encountered with his manner and good humor and in November was granted unconditional freedom by the governor.

Emmett moved to Oklahoma to be near his mother and took a couple of odd jobs in Tulsa before being tapped for a trip to the East Coast with the Tulsa Commercial Club. He was the star of the trip, meeting President Theodore Roosevelt and being hounded by newspaper reporters.

In September 1908 Emmett married Julia Lewis and settled in Bartlesville, Oklahoma. By the end of the year, he was serving as a consultant for a film on the Coffeyville raid to be shown at the 1909 Seattle World's Fair. (The governor who freed Emmett was not thrilled by this spectacle.) The next year he found himself nominated for the Bartlesville city council and touring Oklahoma with the Coffeyville filmmaker, recounting the robberies and giving speeches about the perils of lawbreaking. A new Kansas governor threatened to revoke Emmett's pardon if he continued to make a spectacle of his crimes, but Emmett was not fazed.

By 1911 Emmett was a fulltime showman. He assisted with a new Dalton movie, directed by Jack Kenyon, and made his living with speaking engagements. He made sure to include prisons in his tours, as he was passionate about prison reform and abolishing capital punishment.

In 1918 Emmett published his first book, *Beyond the Law*, and felt compelled to move with Julia to Hollywood. The book was made into a movie—Emmett even acted in this one.

Enthralled with Hollywood, Emmett became the general manager of two film production companies: Southern Feature Film Corporation and Standard Pictures of California, Inc. He also found his way into the construction business—highly lucrative, as Hollywood was exploding at that time. And he made time for politics, in 1920 petitioning the governor of California to commute the death sentence of a sixteen-year-old boy.

> . . . Murder is an act of horror, and one horror cannot be cured by another," Emmett wrote to the governor. "As I once had a life sentence, and from my experience for observation along these lines, I have become unalterably opposed to capital punishment. The aim of society should never be to hurt, but to cure.

The governor commuted the inmate's sentence to life in prison.

Emmett's most successful book, *When the Daltons Rode,* written with Jack Jungmeyer, was published in 1931. Emmett celebrated its release by returning to Kansas, looking every bit the wealthy Hollywood type. He was greeted as a celebrity in Coffeyville, where he ordered markers for his dead brothers' graves and continued his crusade against the death penalty, as noted by a reporter:

> The elderly man who arrived from California bore little resemblance to the 'bad man' of Kansas and Oklahoma pioneer days. Prosperous from his earnings as a building contractor in California, Dalton is here to gather literary material and also to leave at the office of Governor Murray a plea against capital punishment.

A few years later Emmett's health began a downhill slide. In 1937 he suffered a stroke and died not long thereafter at the age of sixty-seven.

In 1940 Hollywood produced the major film *When the Daltons Rode,* which starred Randolph Scott and Kay Francis. The Daltons indeed had become legend, although Bob and Grat never lived to see it.

George "Bitter Creek" Newcomb
Romantic Robber, 1893

"I'm a wild wolf from Bitter Creek, and it's my night to howl," the young cowboy sang. It was his favorite song, and he hummed it every day as he went about his work moving cattle, putting up fence, or tending horses. He sang it to whoever might be listening—cows, dogs, people, no one at all.

"I'm a wild wolf from Bitter Creek, and it's my night to howl," he sang. He wasn't from a place called Bitter Creek at all but rather Fort Scott, Kansas. Still, his affinity for the folk tune earned him the nickname "Bitter Creek."

His real name was George Newcomb, and he was born in 1866 in far eastern Kansas just after the Civil War came to a close. Though his uncle ran one of the largest grocery stores in the state, his own family was poor, and he left home early. In 1878, when a Texas rancher came through Fort Scott selling horses, twelve-year-old Newcomb followed the man back to his Long S Ranch on the Colorado River. His time there earned him another nickname, "Slaughter Kid," though that one didn't stick quite as well as "Bitter Creek."

Newcomb eventually drifted north into Indian Territory, where he gained a reputation as a hard worker for rancher Oscar Halsell. Newcomb had grown into a dark, handsome young man, and he loved women as much as he loved his free, cowboy existence. But when he met a man named Bill Doolin, his life changed forever.

Bill Doolin ran with the Dalton boys, a gang of robbers that had terrorized Kansas and surrounding states for the last two years. No train or bank was safe with them nearby.

Doolin recruited Newcomb into the fold, and in the summer of 1892 the young Kansan joined them for a little train-robbing fun.

One July night the outlaws rode their horses into Adair, a small train stop in Indian Territory, just before the 9:45 train. There they robbed the depot and seized the train. Newcomb kept the passengers at gunpoint to avoid a revolt while the others raided the express car for valuables. Shots flew between the robbers and guards, resulting in injuries for three of the officials but none of the thieves.

Newcomb reveled in his share of the booty. It was much easier money than working on the ranch, that was for sure. Emmett Dalton, one of the outlaw brothers, would later describe Newcomb as a perfect fit for the group—a solid shot with a rifle, good on a horse, and exceedingly reckless.

For the Dalton Gang, it was just another success story in a long list of crimes. Drunk on their seeming invincibility, the Daltons came up with a most ambitious scheme. The men would rob not one but *two* banks in one day—in broad daylight. Plus, their location of choice was Coffeyville, the Daltons' hometown. It was a wildly bold plan that would make history.

The Dalton Gang did make history when they knocked over two banks in Coffeyville on October 5, 1892, but for the wrong reasons. The robbery was a massive failure—four of the robbers ended up dead and another was captured. A sixth gunman was said to have escaped, and it's thought the man was Bill Doolin.

Luckily for Newcomb, he and fellow bandit Charlie Pierce had been left out of the Coffeyville raid and thus lived to see another robbery.

It didn't take long, either.

After the Coffeyville mess, Newcomb, Doolin, and Pierce wanted to make sure the town didn't breathe too large a sigh of relief at the death of their friends. They sent a letter to one of the townspeople who had helped gun down the bank robbers:

> Dear Sir:
> I take the time to tell you and city of Coffeyville that all of the gang ain't dead yet by a hell of a sight and don't you forget it. I would have given all I ever made to have been there on the 5th. There are three of the gang left and we shall come to see you . . . we shall have revenge for your killing of Bob and Grat and the rest . . . You people had no cause to take arms against the gang. The bankers will not help the widows of the men that got killed there and you thought you were playing hell fire when you killed three of us, but your time will soon come when you will go into the grave and pass in your checks . . . So take warning.
> Yours truly,
> DALTON GANG.

News of the ominous letter rattled the town, still reeling from the bloodshed of the failed robbery. The climate of fear reached fever pitch when the Coffeyville mayor received a message by wire from a detective hunting for the remaining outlaws. According to him, a massive group of forty desperadoes—led by Doolin, Newcomb, and Pierce—had just passed Wharton, Indian Territory, en route to Coffeyville. They intended to "wipe out" the entire town, according to the informant.

The town obtained weapons and reinforcements all the way from Kansas City and lit a bonfire in the town square to keep the streets well lit.

The band of outlaws never showed up.

Presumably deterred by Coffeyville's vigilance but still brimming with angry energy to conduct a crime, the surviving gang members instead donned masks at the Caney train station eighteen miles west of Coffeyville. When the train arrived on the Missouri Pacific Railroad tracks at 10:15 p.m., the men were waiting. They climbed onto the train, one of them pointing a gun in the engineer's face, and after a short distance ordered that the express car be quietly disconnected from the rest of the train. As ordered, the engineer moved the express car another half mile down the track. A shot was fired, signaling the others to empty valuables from another car. They sprang into action, forcing a railroad employee—bleeding from a shot in the arm—to unload the safe.

Although the robbers got away, they didn't have much to show for it—around $1,500 at best. Most of the train's valuables had been transferred to another train at Conway Springs. Still, it was a victory for the rebel pack's morale—survivors of the Dalton Gang, they had pulled off their first robbery without a Dalton. The small gang, led by Bill Doolin, would be known as the Doolin Gang, or the Wild Bunch.

Coffeyville remained on alert, news of the nearby heist fueling fears that a murderous posse indeed would emerge. But the Wild Bunch had other matters to tend to.

First they recruited a new man, Oliver Yantis. A thick fellow with a dark face and a dark moustache, he had helped harbor the Dalton Gang after a horse theft several months prior.

Hiding and feeding the bandits, Yantis's sister had fallen for the handsome Newcomb, and Yantis himself had fallen for the outlaw lifestyle. Now Yantis would fill in for Charlie Pierce on a trek to Garden City, a hundred miles away.

It was late October, and the air was crisp. They arrived in Garden City on the twenty-first, staying in the Ohio House while they scouted the area over the next week. They liked the looks of a little town called Spearville. Less than twenty miles east of Dodge City, the place was a stop on the Santa Fe Railroad and had just two hundred residents, hardly enough to mount a real fight against armed invaders. On the twenty-ninth the outlaws were spotted on an area ranch sporting copious numbers of weapons. Then, on November 1, it was time to get serious.

The weather had turned cold, and most of the people of Spearville were holed up indoors. Doolin, Newcomb and Yantis rode right up to the Ford County Bank. Doolin and Newcomb left their thoroughbreds with Yantis and entered the bank. In a matter of minutes Newcomb filled a bag with $1,697 while Doolin stuck his Winchester rifle in the face of physically handicapped cashier J. R. Baird. Newcomb and Doolin rejoined Yantis and their horses, fired a few victorious shots, and rode away. They encountered a small pack of locals who exchanged a few shots, none of which struck anything but air.

When County Sheriff Chalkey Beeson caught wind of the robbery, he led a posse southeast along the river.

The menacing trio was spotted a number of times traversing the country south of Dodge, and they ultimately split up to avoid detection. Doolin and Newcomb would follow different routes but meet up back at their Cimarron hideout, while Yantis would go to his sister's home in Orlando, Kansas.

Sheriff Beeson gave up the trail and sent postcards to nearby towns and train stations, offering a $450 reward for capture of the thieves and warning people to be on the lookout for crisp, new $5 bills that had made it into Newcomb's bag. Beeson described the three suspects, whose names he didn't yet know: The "small dark complexioned man 23 years old, small, very dark mustached and dark clothes" was Yantis; the "medium sized man, sandy complexioned, short beard, light hat and clothes" was Doolin; and the "dark man, 25 years old, medium size dark mustache" was Bitter Creek Newcomb.

A couple weeks later, the sheriff got a break. A Stillwater, Indian Territory, man believed he had seen the small, dark man in question. Sheriff Beeson sent a Garden City man who had seen the trio at the Ohio House during their scouting week. When the man found Yantis at a home near Stillwater, he recognized him but didn't let on. Still, Yantis sensed that something was amiss, shifting nervously and keeping his hand near his holster. In a week or so, Sheriff Beeson arrived with authority to make an arrest in Indian Territory, far outside his normal jurisdiction.

In the early morning fog, the lawman and his aides reached the homestead where Yantis was staying. When Yantis finally walked out of the house, Beeson yelled. Yantis grabbed his pistol and fired. His sister, Newcomb's old flame, ran out to try to stop the madness, but it was too late. The lawmen had gunned Yantis down, and the novice outlaw slowly bled to death. Bills from the Ford County Bank were found in his wallet, confirming his identity, and the sheriff collected a reward. Once again, though, Doolin, Newcomb, and Pierce remained at large.

Over the winter months, the Wild Bunch found a couple more able outlaws by the names of Tulsa Jack and Dynamite Dick. In June 1893 all five donned masks and hit a train just west of Cimarron. This train they mounted with particular flourish, swinging down from a bridge as the locomotive passed underneath.

The outlaws moved past the Kansas borders into Indian Territory, holding up trains and vulnerable travelers in Bartlesville, Ingalls, Sacred Heart, and Dover. They struck wherever and whomever they pleased. The Dalton Gang was dead and, thanks to the wiliness of Newcomb and Doolin, the Wild Bunch was the new gang to fear.

By 1895 Bitter Creek had a $5,000 prize on his head, though his true identity—George Newcomb—remained unknown. He'd spent the last few years successfully evading the law, amassing wealth by robbery and killing men who got in the way. But he was still a young man with a soft spot for women.

Newcomb met a pretty teenage girl named Rosa Dunn at a country dance in Cimarron, and the two developed a romance. They made a good-looking pair; Rosa would become known as the "the Rose of Cimarron." Newcomb and Pierce also made friends with Dunn's brothers. The Dunns provided a hideout, while the outlaws shared their considerable loot.

But on May 2, 1895, the Dunn ranch would go from a safe haven to a deadly trap. When Newcomb and Pierce arrived that day to see Rosa and collect a large sum of money owed by her brothers, the Dunn boys turned on them, unloading lead into the two outlaws and tossing their bodies into a wagon bound for Guthrie. When Newcomb somehow gasped another breath the next morning, he got another bullet for his trouble and was finally dead. The Dunns would have their reward, in the process putting it on the record that their lovely sister had known nothing of their plans.

Newcomb's body was identified a few days later, sending his hometown of Fort Scott into shock. A former resident told an area paper that the people of Fort Scott would "learn with horror that the little pale faced, well mannered boy, George Newcomb, who played around the streets and about his uncle's store, was no other than the daring highwayman, Slaughter Kid . . . It hardly seems credible that a boy surrounded as he was with influential friends, a kind, honorable and industrious father could go so astray."

The Bird Man of Kansas
Leavenworth, 1912

Inmate number 8154, a curious man with a gaunt face, sat alone in his cell. The dimly lit room, with its cold, austere walls, was twelve by six feet, into which were crammed a cot, toilet, and washbowl. The man was taller than the cell was wide. A bit of sunlight came in through the bars of a tiny window. Other than the bugs that inhabited his space, the man had no companions. Solitary confinement. But, he would say, that was OK with him. He hadn't had much use for people since they dealt him a punishment that, to hear him tell it, far outreached his crimes.

Sometimes the man was allowed to leave his cell and walk around the prison yard for a bit of exercise. There, getting a glimpse of the big Kansas sky, he might have reflected on the incidents that led him to Leavenworth Federal Penitentiary.

In 1909, at the age of nineteen, Robert Stroud already had been on his own for nearly a third of his life, having run away at age thirteen from a home life he despised in Seattle. He made his way to Cordova, Alaska, a frontier town. There he met a thirty-six-year-old dance hall entertainer and prostitute, Kitty O'Brien, and the two began an affair. They moved to Juneau. Life wasn't too bad. He was broke, but he had a woman and he was young. He was free.

According to Stroud, that all changed when Charlie Von Dahmer entered the picture. Von Dahmer was an acquaintance of sorts who might have had romantic designs on O'Brien.

135

One day he savagely beat the woman, Stroud claimed. To avenge O'Brien, Stroud took her gun to Von Dahmer's home and waited for him to arrive. When he did, Stroud shot him to death. Then he turned himself in.

To be sure, men had gone free after far lesser crimes in frontier towns at the turn of the twentieth century. But Stroud ended up with a twelve-year sentence on McNeil Island, a rough prison near Tacoma, Washington, where inmates wore stripes, weren't allowed to speak, and faced tough punishment for rule-breaking. Stroud learned that the hard way. When a fellow prisoner reported him for stealing food, Stroud stabbed him with a kitchen knife—the incident cost him his chance at parole. About a year after going to prison, he was sent in 1912 from McNeil Island to a prison in an ocean of Kansas prairie—Leavenworth.

Leavenworth was an even harsher environment. The food was barely edible—stews of questionable meats and textures. A wrong step might result in being clubbed, chained to a twenty-five-pound ball, or thrown into "the hole." After seven years there, Stroud was suicidal.

In 1916 a purpose for living arrived in the form of a fruit basket. It was from his long-lost brother, who had made a long journey from Alaska to visit him. However, Stroud was enraged to find that his brother had been sent away because it was the weekend. Dangerously embittered, Stroud rebelled against the "silence system" at dinner, grumbling about the injustice of his brother's thwarted visit. A guard, Andrew Turner, made a note of his bad behavior.

Fearing that Turner might report him—and thus ruin any remaining chance at seeing his brother—Stroud cracked. The next day at lunch, he found the guard in the mess hall, pulled a knife from his coat, and stabbed the man in the chest. To the shock of hundreds of inmates, Turner fell to the floor, spurting blood.

At the subsequent trial, seven of those inmates gladly testified against Stroud in exchange for pardons for their own crimes. Stroud was found guilty but appealed on a technicality. He was found guilty again and appealed again. Finally, in a third trial he was sentenced to hang for the murder of the Leavenworth guard.

Stroud's mother pleaded for her son's life and, a week before his scheduled execution, President Woodrow Wilson commuted the sentence to life in prison.

That's how Robert Stroud found himself in solitary confinement at the age of thirty. He would live in that dank Leavenworth cell for the next three decades—although before too long, he would have more than cockroaches for friends.

While strolling the prison yard one day during a brief release from his cell for exercise (alone of course), Stroud found two baby sparrows under a fallen tree limb. Heartened by the chance to interact with another living creature, he brought the birds back to his cell. He spent hours—and he had plenty of free ones—playing with the birds and teaching them tricks, such as rolling over and playing dead. Somehow he could commune with the sparrows. He understood them, and they brought him joy. Stroud might have been behind bars, but he had found his calling. The bitter, dangerous inmate was dead, and the Bird Man was born.

By the time Stroud reached his thirties, he had undergone a transformation—from emotional and volatile to placid and

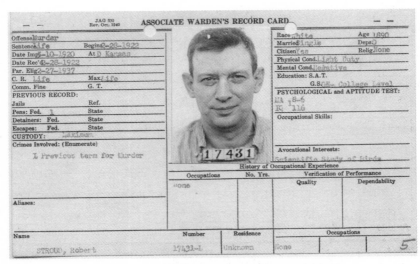

Robert Stroud's prison record in Leavenworth, Kansas, including a note of his interest in "scientific study of birds." *National Archives and Records Administration*

proud—and so had Leavenworth. The prison had been rebuilt—its own inmates providing the labor—into a 366,000-square-foot castle with six floors, 1,200 cells, an inmate radio station, a gym, a movie theater, a chapel, and a death chamber. None of that concerned Stroud, though. He was in the basement, alone, bending his six-foot-three frame over in study, obsessing over birds through a pair of old-fashioned glasses.

Stroud had moved on from sparrows to canaries, and his cell housed three hundred of them in cages handmade from sliced cigar boxes. He took a particular interest in the birds that fell sick. He'd try various methods of curing them, dissecting the dead ones with his fingernails and then painstakingly document their symptoms, progress, and demise. Stroud found that the books he could access were woefully superficial and didn't do justice to the complexities of his beloved canaries. Thus he seized on the idea of education for the first time in his life, borrowing from the prison library books on chemistry, medicine, bacteria, pharmacology, and even English grammar.

Soon, having gotten his hands on an old typewriter, he was a regular contributor to canary journals nationwide. He wrote letters back and forth with thousands of canary lovers and breeders. He sold some of the birds he raised with his mother's help and supported her with the earnings. Meanwhile, he continued to document his observations ("Unlike mammals, birds have air cavities in the principal bones . . .") and diseases such as baldness, molt, and rickets, even illustrating his own text. The project would culminate in the publication of a respected work, *Diseases of Canaries,* in 1933.

Stroud faced a major roadblock in his endeavors, though. In 1931 prison authorities thought he was enjoying himself too much and gave him two months to wrap up the bird operation and get rid of his feathered friends.

Stroud wrote a letter to the feds outlining for them the service he was providing to bird lovers everywhere, imbuing his plea with a comparison between himself and his caged birds. He put the letter into the hands of middle-aged widow and bird fancier Della May Jones, who succeeded in circulating it among bird fanatics across the country. Soon hundreds of letters poured into congressmen and the Federal Bureau of Prisons, imploring them to let the Bird Man continue his work.

The bureau's newly appointed assistant director, James Bennett, was given the reins on handling the situation. He sought a compromise with Stroud, who now held a powerful upper hand due to public sentiment. But Stroud wouldn't cooperate. In the end he walked away with more than he had to begin with—two cells connected by a door, lab equipment, and electrical outlets to power them. Oh, and a new pair of glasses. To allow for all this, Stroud was now categorized as a "special prisoner of the Bureau."

Stroud was back in business. Wesleyan University gave him a microscope, and Stroud meticulously constructed his own microtome with scraps of metal and glass for slicing animal tissues to examine. With Della May Jones's help, he even sold prison-formulated concoctions with names like Stroud's Effervescent Bird Salts, Stroud's Special Prescription, and Stroud's Salts No. 1.

The bureau, embarrassed by Stroud's power play, retaliated by limiting his correspondence and halting his contributions to magazines. Wanting to be done with him and his feather-filled, poop-laden cell altogether, they started the process of sending him elsewhere—to the federal prison on Alcatraz Island.

Stroud caught wind of this and devised a plan to stay with his birds. After poring over old law books, Stroud concluded that he couldn't be sent away if he were married. Enter Della May Jones, once again. The two married, and Stroud remained in Kansas. The infuriated prison officials banned him from seeing Jones, but that wasn't the point. He would see his birds every day.

After Stroud had spent thirty years at Leavenworth, James Bennett—by now director of the Federal Bureau of Prisons—was ready to be done with the bird problem. He was sick of the media attention Stroud received and went out of his way to obscure Stroud's records and block direct access to the prisoner.

Bennett finally succeeded in relocating Stroud to Alcatraz in 1942. That same year, the inmate published *Stroud's Digest on the Diseases of Birds* after twenty years of studies with canaries in his Leavenworth cell.

By now the Bird Man was fifty-two, suffered from arthritis, and hadn't committed a violent act in twenty-six years. He was distraught at losing his avian friends but proud even in this lost battle. He would write that he could have long ago been granted parole—for which he became eligible in 1937—if he'd only sucked up to Bennett, but he wasn't interested.

"I am neither a moron nor a sycophant, the only types they conceive worthy, but a man of strong character who in fifty years has not been broken and who cannot be broken," Stroud wrote. "I am still Prometheus and I can endure . . . to the end if necessary." He was aging into an old man, but his ego was as robust as ever.

That ego got a real treat when author Thomas Gaddis wrote Stroud's story in *The Birdman of Alcatraz* in 1955. Bennett, who had failed to stop the book's publication, called the sympathetic tale a "pack of lies," but the book was a success. Stroud received letters of encouragement from around the world.

Three years later, Twentieth Century Fox attempted to make a movie based on the book. Bennett managed to curb that initial effort, but the studio pressed on, even consulting with Stroud for artistic guidance. Stroud wrote to the Hollywood executives that he shouldn't be portrayed as a hero or a genius.

"He is neither," Stroud wrote, waxing dramatically on his own character. "He is an unfortunate human being who got off in life on the wrong foot, almost from birth; a criminal, a murderer, a man who has done many evil, shameful and terrible things and has suffered terrible punishments. He is a pronounced egotist. The one outstanding thing about him is that he has been a fighter from the day of birth. He has always fought against heartbreaking odds and without the advantages of preparation for the battle of life. So . . . though Stroud is as devoid of conventional morals as a chicken is of teeth, his story contains one great moral lesson: Man can die, but he can never be a slave until he himself accepts slavery."

Stroud wrote two more manuscripts at Alcatraz—an autobiography and a historical discourse on the federal prison system. Then, in 1959, due in part to public outcry over Stroud's unusually long solitary confinement, he was moved to much more pleasant conditions in a federal prison hospital in Springfield, Missouri. By 1962 *The Birdman of Alcatraz* was a hit film starring Burt Lancaster, and Stroud was a grouchy, seventy-two-year-old prisoner with failing kidneys, numerous publications, and the self-taught ability to read Latin and French. When Stroud died in 1963 at the age of seventy-three, he had spent more than fifty years incarcerated—more than forty of which were in solitary confinement. For much of that time of course he was hardly alone—he had hundreds of feathered friends.

Bad Sermon
Muscotah, 1915

The small-town preacher held sheets of paper in his hands. On the paper was handwritten one of his recent sermons about good and evil. The writing paper had a new purpose, though. The preacher folded it, wrapped it, and bent it until the dynamite was tightly packed and completely hidden.

The preacher, George Morton Field, was a wealthy man, at least by the standards of the tiny town of Muscotah. The town, in the northeast corner of the state, looked to Field for its economic foundation. He had helped finance the construction of the church in which he preached every Sunday. They looked to him for inspiration as well. Parish members strove to match Pastor Field's stringent moral code.

So when Field took special notice of a young church choir member named Gertie Day, she could hardly refuse his attentions. Their illicit relations blew up in Field's face, however, when Day—twenty years younger than he was—revealed that she was pregnant.

The solution was clear-cut enough: Field would give Day $2,000 to leave town and never speak of their affair. Day agreed to the offer. They would meet, and money would change hands, at the church.

After the plan had been settled upon, though, Field began to fret. What if Gertie Day didn't keep her end of the bargain? She could easily take the small fortune and then share the sordid tale with the whole town. Or she could continue to hang the incident over his head for a lifetime, blackmailing him for more money whenever she saw fit. And what about the baby who might grow up to bear a resemblance to him? The current situation held too many dangerous unknowns.

So Field traveled to nearby Kansas City to purchase a few sticks of dynamite. He wrapped them in the sermon he had delivered the previous Sunday and hustled to the church, where Day would be waiting for her payment. Instead of going inside with an envelope full of money, however, he placed his homemade bomb beneath the church, lit the wick, and quietly fled.

The dynamite did its job. Gertie Day and her unborn baby were dead. As for the church, it was leveled.

The Atchison County sheriff poked around the gutted church. Among the ashes and debris he found bits of dynamite and, most interestingly, scraps of paper onto which were written Pastor Field's recent sermon.

The sheriff asked around and discovered that the pastor had made a trip to Kansas City and that, on said trip, he purchased dynamite and wires from a hardware store.

Field was arrested and convicted of murdering Gertie Day. He was sentenced to life in the state penitentiary at Lansing, where he remained until his death in 1926.

Stella Hyman
Poison on the Prairie, 1919

Stella Hyman was pregnant with her nephew's child.

It was 1919 in rural Kansas, and Hyman was worried about the bastard baby growing beneath her cotton dress. What would people say? She desperately wanted to marry the father of her child, Lee Bunch. She wasn't so concerned about the attitude toward incest among her fellow residents of Lincoln County, on the windswept prairie of central Kansas. But she was worried about having a baby out of wedlock.

Hyman regularly visited the Bunch residence, inhabited by Ed, wife Lizzie—Hyman's sister—and their grown children, Lee and Nancy. Hyman was in her late twenties and Lee Bunch a bit younger when they had a romp during the cold winter months of early 1919. When she discovered that she was pregnant, she announced her situation to the family who, according to her, were none too pleased.

Hyman's sister, Lizzie, was appalled at the situation. Her son had impregnated her sister. It was shameful. And now the pair wanted to get married? Lizzie and her husband responded by treating Hyman coldly. No, she certainly would not be marrying their son, Lee, bastard baby or none.

Hyman begged, but the Bunches refused. According to Hyman, they berated her, struck her, and generally abused her for creating such a miserable, embarrassing situation.

Their daughter, Nancy, also felt hostile toward Hyman. One day, her anger boiling into violence as she shared the kitchen with her pregnant aunt, Nancy grabbed a knife and sliced Hyman's hand with it.

For Hyman—pregnant, unmarried, and under attack—this was the final straw.

In the middle of July in 1919, the powerful summer was burning the dry Kansas landscape and Stella Hyman was burning with hatred for Ed, Lizzie, and Nancy. She had a plan to escape her miserable family life, and she shared it with Lee: flypaper.

The dark-brown, insect-killing product was rife with poison, enough to kill far more than flies. Lizzie kept some in the house. It would be easy as pie.

Tomato pie, to be exact.

Lizzie had just baked with the summer bounty of tomatoes. The pie sat in the kitchen in the hot morning hours, waiting to be eaten for lunch. Before everyone sat down to eat, Hyman crept into the kitchen and pulled a piece of flypaper from the cabinet. She ran water over the flypaper, collecting the poisonous runoff. She then poured the water onto a piece of tomato pie.

Around eleven o'clock, the Bunch family came in to eat. Young Nancy grabbed the tainted piece of pie and gobbled it up.

Within an hour, Nancy was very ill. Later in the day, the local physician, Dr. Higgins, made a house call. Nancy remained in bed, struggling against the mysterious pains in her stomach.

The next day, Nancy remained weak and bedridden, but she was still alive. Aunt Stella saw that she needed to continue the dosage if her flypaper scheme was to have its intended effect. For the next two weeks she fed a secret regimen of flypaper poison to her despised niece, dribbling it into the girl's lemonade, milk, water, tea, and coffee. Nancy ingested the poison several times a day. But she would not die.

Hyman told her incestuous lover, Lee, that her plan was in motion and that she would now turn her sights on his mother, Lizzie.

Hyman poured the poison into her sister's coffee and other beverages. Within hours, Lizzie Bunch was sick. Again, Dr. Higgins visited the house, by now raising his eyebrows over the household's mysterious ailments. For the next few days, Hyman continued to poison her sister until she was taken to the larger nearby town of Salina for medical treatment. She died there on August 1.

Lincoln County Sheriff Sim Hoover and Marshal M. J. Driscoll noted the death, which struck them as suspicious. They asked a few questions and poked around the Bunch residence a bit. But, they reasoned, people fell ill all the time. It wasn't real cause for alarm.

For Edward Bunch, however, the situation was supremely alarming. His wife was dead, his young daughter had been sick in bed for weeks, and his sister-in-law was pregnant with his son's child. He returned from Salina and his wife's burial an emotionally broken man, and he had a sense that Hyman was behind all of his woes. Hyman would claim that Ed refused to let her leave his home and that she overheard his plan to murder her with the loaded revolver he kept in the home.

I might as well kill him as to have him kill me, Hyman thought, as she would later recount. So, just days after Lizzie Bunch's death, Hyman added an unhealthy seasoning of fly-poison to Ed Bunch's coffee at dinnertime.

By noon the next day, Ed returned home, sick. He couldn't afford yet another house call from Dr. Higgins, to whom he owed money, so another physician, Dr. Kerr, treated him. It was no use, though. In the days to come, Hyman continued to doctor up her brother-in-law's coffee. Ed Bunch died on August 14, two weeks after his wife's passing.

Now Sheriff Hoover and Marshal Driscoll were on the job. Convinced that foul play had been involved in the Bunch deaths, they hovered around the family home, pestering Stella and Lee with questions. Meanwhile, young Nancy—newly orphaned—remained in bed with no indication of improvement.

The months passed in Lincoln County, Kansas. Stella Hyman's baby came into the world, the air turned cold, and winter swept the flat land. By springtime of the next year, Sheriff Hoover, Marshal Driscoll, and County Attorney M. J. Healy were convinced that Stella Hyman had murdered her sister and brother-in-law. But without any hard evidence, they brought her in on other another charge: incest.

With Hyman in custody, the officials badgered the woman about the Bunch family until finally, on May 20, 1920, she confessed to the murders. Lee Bunch then was hauled in to another cell at the Lincoln County jail, charged with being an accessory to the murder of his parents.

The revelation of the crime rocked the small community. The *Lincoln Sentinel* called it "one of the most sensational murder cases in the history of Lincoln County." The paper reported that Hyman had denied all accusations until finally snapping under interrogation by County Attorney Healy.

"She stoutly maintained her innocence until Mr. Healy, by tangling her statements, led her to divulge the whole sordid tale," the newspaper stated.

Hyman, then a twenty-nine-year-old mother of an infant child, related the events in a chillingly calm manner.

"Mr. Bunch, Mrs. Bunch, and Nancy Bunch always treated me mean and they would not let Lee marry me," Hyman said under oath. "I poisoned all three of them. I used flypaper. It was poison off of a piece of dark brown fly-poison that Mrs. Bunch had in the house."

Hyman went on to claim that she had experienced some anxiety over her actions, but she remained matter-of-fact in the telling.

"I am making this statement of my own accord and free will and under no threat of any kind whatsoever," Hyman said, "but I cannot stand to keep this confession any more as it is bothering me and has been on my mind ever since I have done it. I don't know now why I did it. The only reason I can give is because they were so mean to me."

The same day, Lee Bunch confessed to his part in the killings. No, he had never held the dripping fly paper over a cup of coffee, but he had known of Hyman's intentions and heard about her actions involving his mother, father, and sister. In his confession he stated that "at all of said times, said Lee Bunch never told her not to do it, and after all of said events and at no time prior to this date has said Lee Bunch ever informed any of the officers as to what he knew of the circumstances connected with the death of said parties, either before or after the administration of poison."

The people of Lincoln County were distraught not just over the murders but also over the pitiful case of Nancy Bunch, who had "so patiently borne her unwarranted sufferings, does not know of the confession." The young girl, the *Lincoln Sentinel* reported, "has been confined to her bed since she received the dose of poison early in July last year and at times has been near death's door. Through it all, however, the aunt and confessed murderer has maintained a calm indifference. Nancy Bunch, physicians say, will be a helpless invalid the rest of her life."

The paper went on to describe Hyman as a "shrewd, designing creature" who with Lee Bunch made a "loathsome pair" and "illegal offspring." The consensus was that the two were lucky so many months had passed since the Bunch deaths, as news of Hyman's involvement might have sparked a vigilante mob when passions were higher.

The day after her initial confession, Hyman further outlined her crimes to County Attorney Healy, revealing the shocking extent of the poisonings—two to three times per day for each of her three victims. When she stood trial for first-degree murder two weeks later, it was a fast procedure. Just twelve hours passed from the first testimony in the morning to the jury's guilty verdict returned that evening.

Lee Bunch fared better. He was found not guilty as a murder accomplice but did plead guilty to incest and was sentenced to prison time. Within days, on an early summer day nearly a year after Hyman pulled the flypaper from the cabinet,

Bunch would join his aunt on a ride with Sheriff Hoover to the foreboding Kansas State Penitentiary in Lansing.

Hyman was to spend the rest of her life there, and Bunch was looking at a seven-year sentence. But the two were unfazed. "Neither of the prisoners seemed much concerned over the momentous trip," the local paper stated.

Hyman had escaped the emotional imprisonment of her domestic life, but now she faced a much more literal confinement. And her infant child, that "illegal offspring," was orphaned, stripped of its parents as Nancy Bunch was of hers.

Bibliography

Bushwhackers

McPherson, James M. *The Civil War Battlefield Guide*, 2nd ed. Boston: Houghton Mifflin Harcourt Publishing Company, 1998.

Smith, Robert Barr. *The Last Hurrah of the James-Younger Gang*. Norman, OK: University of Oklahoma Press, 2001.

Stiles, T. J. *Jesse James: Last Rebel of the Civil War*. New York: Knopf, 2002.

Ward, Stephanie Francis. "The Lawyer Who Took on Jesse James . . . and Won," *ABA Journal*, No. 94; March 2008, p. 40.

Johnny Hardin

Hardin, John Wesley. *The Life of John Wesley Hardin*. Norman, OK: University of Oklahoma Press, 1977.

Metz, Leon C. *John Wesley Hardin: Dark Angel of Texas*. Norman, OK: University of Oklahoma Press, 1998.

Phil Coe

Barra, Allen. *Inventing Wyatt Earp: His Life and Many Legends*. Lincoln, NE: University of Nebraska Press, 2009.

Heavey, Bill, and David E. Petzal. "The Gunslingers," *Field &
Stream*, Vol. 112, No. 7, pp. 66–70, 2007.

Patterson, Richard M. *Historical Atlas of the Outlaw West.*
Boulder, CO: Johnson Books, 1984.

Walton, William. *The Life and Adventures of Ben Thompson,
the Famous Texan.* Austin, TX: Steck, 1956.

The Newton Massacre

Miller, Nyle, and Joseph W. Snell. *Why the West Was
Wild: A Contemporary Look at the Antics of Some Highly
Publicized Kansas Cowtown Personalities.* Norman, OK:
University of Oklahoma Press, 2003.

O'Neal, Bill. *Encyclopedia of Western Gunfighters.* Norman,
OK: University of Oklahoma Press, 1991.

Kate Bender

Nash, Jay Robert. *The Great Pictorial History of World Crime.*
Lanham, MD: The Scarecrow Press, 2004.

The New York Times. "The Bender Family: A New Theory
in Explanation of the Sudden Disappearance of the
Murderous Family," November 30, 1876.

The New York Times. "The Benders in Custody," July 31,
1880.

The New York Times. "The Alleged Benders Held,"
November 21, 1889.

The New York Times. "Says They're Not the Benders,"
January 12, 1890.

Bibliography

The New York Times. "Said to Be the Benders," July 24, 1901.

The New York Times. "Dying Man Clears the Bender
  Mystery," July 12, 1908.

The New York Times. "Kate Bender Dead," May 6, 1910.

Wood, Fern M. *The Benders: Keepers of the Devil's Inn.* Fern
  M. Wood, 1992.

Young, Richard, and Judy Dockrey. *Outlaw Tales: Legends,
  Myths, and Folklore From America's Middle Border.*
  Atlanta: August House, 1992.

Ben Thompson

O'Neal, Bill. *Encyclopedia of Western Gunfighters.* Norman,
  OK: University of Oklahoma Press, 1991.

Robinson, Charles. *American Frontier Lawmen, 1850–1930.*
  Oxford: Osprey Publishing, 2005.

Billy Brooks

Coke, Tom S. *Caldwell: Kansas Border Cow Town.*
  Westminster, MD: Heritage Books, 2005.

Miller, Nyle, and Joseph W. Snell. *Why the West Was
  Wild: A Contemporary Look at the Antics of Some Highly
  Publicized Kansas Cowtown Personalities.* Norman, OK:
  University of Oklahoma Press, 2003.

Bibliography

Dirty Dave Rudabaugh

Marriott, Barbara. *Outlaw Tales of New Mexico.* Guilford,
    CT: Globe Pequot Press, 2007.
Smith, Robert Barr. *Tough Towns: True Tales from the Gritty
    Streets of the Old West.* Guilford, CT: Globe Pequot Press,
    2006.

Big Nose Kate

Loy, R. Philip. *Westerns in a Changing America, 1955–2000.*
    Jefferson, NC: McFarland & Company, 2004.
Marks, Paula Mitchel. *And Die in the West: The story of O.K.
    Corral Gunfight.* Norman, OK: University of Oklahoma
    Press, 1996.
Rutter, Michael. *Upstairs Girls: Prostitution in the American
    West.* Helena, MT: Farcountry Press, 2005.

The Masterson Brothers

Asfar, Dan. *Outlaws and Lawmen of the West, Vol. II.* Renton,
    WA: Lone Pine Publishing Company, 2001.
Butler, Ken. *More Oklahoma Renegades.* Gretna, LA: Pelican
    Publishing Company, 2007.
Miller, Nyle H., and Joseph W. Snell. *Great Gunfighters of the
    Kansas Cowtowns, 1867–1886.* Lincoln, NE: Bison Books,
    1963.

Bibliography

Nash, Jay Robert. *Encyclopedia of Western Lawmen and Outlaws*. New York: Da Capo Press, 1994.

O'Neal, Bill. *Encyclopedia of Western Gunfighters*. Norman, OK: University of Oklahoma Press, 1979.

Rosa, Joseph G. *The Gunfighter, Man or Myth*. Norman, OK: University of Oklahoma Press, 1969.

Shirley, Glenn. *West of Hell's Fringe*. Norman, OK: University of Oklahoma Press, 1978.

Time-Life Books and Roberta Conlan, eds. *The Wild West*. New York: Warner Books, 1993.

Luke Short

Metz, Leon Claire. *The Shooters*. El Paso, TX: Mangan Books, 1976.

Miller, Nyle H., and Joseph W. Snell. *Great Gunfighters of the Kansas Cowtowns, 1867–1886*. Lincoln, NE: Bison Books, 1963.

Nash, Jay Robert. *Encyclopedia of Western Lawmen and Outlaws*. New York: Da Capo Press, 1994.

O'Neal, Bill. *Encyclopedia of Western Gunfighters*. Norman, OK: University of Oklahoma Press, 1979.

Rosa, Joseph G. *The Gunfighter, Man or Myth*. Norman, OK: University of Oklahoma Press, 1969.

Shirley, Glenn. *West of Hell's Fringe*. Norman, OK: University of Oklahoma Press, 1978.

Bibliography

Henry Brown

Coke, Tom S. *Old West Justice in Belle Plaine, Kansas.* Bowie, MD: Heritage Books, 2002.

O'Neal, Bill. *Encyclopedia of Western Gunfighters.* Norman, OK: University of Oklahoma Press, 1991.

Dave Mather

Asfar, Dan. *Outlaws and Lawmen of the West, Vol. II.* Renton, WA: Lone Pine Publishing Company, 2001.

Metz, Leon Claire. *The Shooters.* El Paso, TX: Mangan Books, 1976.

Miller, Nyle H., and Joseph W. Snell. *Great Gunfighters of the Kansas Cowtowns, 1867–1886.* Lincoln, NE: Bison Books, 1963.

Nash, Jay Robert. *Encyclopedia of Western Lawmen and Outlaws.* New York: Da Capo Press, 1994.

O'Neal, Bill. *Encyclopedia of Western Gunfighters.* Norman, OK: University of Oklahoma Press, 1979.

Rosa, Joseph G. *The Gunfighter, Man or Myth.* Norman, OK: University of Oklahoma Press, 1969.

Time-Life Books and Roberta Conlan, eds. *The Wild West.* New York: Warner Books, 1993.

Bibliography

Emmett Dalton

Galveston Daily News. "The Dalton Gang Has Been Exterminated," October 6, 1892.

The Independence Star and Kansan. October 7, 1892.

The Independence Star and Kansan. October 28, 1892.

The Independence Star and Kansan. March 10, 1893.

The Kansas City Star. November 3, 1907.

The Kansas City Star. September 7, 1920.

The Kansas City Star. April 29, 1931.

The Kansas City Times. October 27, 1892.

The New York Times. "To Surpass Jesse James," October 7, 1892, p. 5.

Ohnick, Nancy. *The Dalton Gang and Their Family Ties.* Meade, KS: Ohnick Enterprises, 2005.

Smith, Robert Barr. *Outlaw Tales of Oklahoma.* Guilford, CT: Morris Book Publishing, 2008.

Wellman, Paul I. *A Dynasty of Western Outlaws.* Lincoln, NE: University of Nebraska Press, 1986.

White, Richard. "Outlaw Gangs of the Middle Border: American Social Bandits," *Western Historical Quarterly 12,* October 1981, pp. 387–408.

George "Bitter Creek" Newcomb

O'Neal, Bill. *Encyclopedia of Western Gunfighters.* Norman, OK: University of Oklahoma Press, 1991.

Rutter, Michael. *Bedside Book of Bad Girls: Outlaw Women of the American West.* Helena, MT: Farcountry Press, 2008.

Bibliography

Shirley, Glenn. *West of Hell's Fringe*. Norman, OK:
University of Oklahoma Press, 1990.

The Bird Man of Kansas

LaMaster, Kenneth M. *U.S. Penitentiary Leavenworth*. Mount
Pleasant, SC: Arcadia Publishing, 2008.
O'Neil, Paul. "Prodigious Intellect In Solitary," *Life*, April 11,
1960, p.p. 140–154.

Bad Sermon

Grout, Pam. *Kansas Curiosities*. Guilford, CT: Globe Pequot
Press, 2007.

Stella Hyman

The Lincoln Sentinel. "Stella Hyman Tells of Murdering
Two," May 13, 1920.
The Lincoln Sentinel. "Stella Hyman Found Guilty," May 27,
1920.
The Lincoln Sentinel. "Hyman and Bunch to Lansing," June 3,
1920.
The New York Times. "Woman Confesses to Poisoning Two,"
May 12, 1920.

Index

Index

161

Index

Index

Index

Index

About the Authors

Sarah Smarsh is a freelance writer and fifth-generation Kansan. She is a fellow of the Center for Kansas Studies and the author of *It Happened In Kansas* (Globe Pequot). She currently lives in northeast Kansas.

Robert Barr Smith is a retired colonel, US Army, and emeritus professor of law at the University of Oklahoma. He is the author of eighteen books and over a hundred magazine articles, mostly in Western and military history. His recent books for TwoDot include *Outlaw Tales of Oklahoma*; *Bad Blood: The Families Who Made the West Wild*; *Tough Towns: True Tales from the Gritty Streets of the Old West*; *The Outlaws: Tales of Bad Guys Who Shaped the Wild West*; and *Outlaw Women: America's Most Notorious Daughters, Wives, and Mothers*. He lives and writes in the Ozark hills of southern Missouri and is a frequent lecturer on the West.